A Beginner's Guide to Astrological Interpretation

Joyce Levine

Vizualizations

Other works by Joyce Levine published by
Vizualizations include meditation tapes:
    Self-Help Series:
        Meditation
        Creative Visualization
        Releasing Anger and Resentment
    Astrology Series:
        Pluto
        Neptune
        Uranus
        Saturn.

First Published by Joyce Levine in 1992

Vizualizations
2353 Massachusetts Avenue #91
Cambridge, Ma 02140
617-354-7075

Library of Congress Catalog No. 95-090114

ISBN 1-885856-09-1

Cover Design by Artichoke Graphics

Table of Contents

ACKNOWLEDGEMENTS

A special thanks goes to Lorraine Welsh for her help in editing this book and to Alphee Lavoie and Carol Lavoie who helped me run off the first edition on their copying machine.

FOREWORD

At the time this book is going to press, the planet Pluto recently went into Sagittarius and the planet Uranus will soon enter its own sign Aquarius. What does all of this signify? Well, it's perhaps the most exciting time of our history. These planetary shifts into these signs are the "signs of the times" that herald the long awaited time for our society when trusts and tenets for us to live by will finally take their rightful place.

In the 90's we've witnessed a waive of consciousness that brought us to where we are today, which is light years ahead of previous decades. And now there is another impetus that is spurring the growth of consciousness even more. We've seen so many "old age wisdoms" in "New Age" products, phrases, and concepts that are now counted as regular norms of the established institutions of our society. The global consciousness, particularly in the countries of power, have wisely stopped to reconsider just where we are headed and shifted tactics in life styles. New at it as we are, we are talking the talk and trying to walk the walk of Awareness.

With this as the key concept toward which are rapidly growing the oldest map of awareness, astrology, is now becoming recognized with high honors as the most useful tool to help bring about this awareness for improvement for both individual and social lifestyles. Astrology has grown and changed so much in its approach from fatalistic orientation to one of unlocking true understanding of behaviors and motivations as well as offering the guidance to make changes in oneself. Today we see astrology being used in the way in which I feel it was always meant to be...that of educating us all and providing us with the awareness to create our futures.

With awareness as the key to our future, the knowledge and wisdom of astrology needs to be preserved and presented in such a way that we can continue to pass it on to our future generations. I remember when I first began to study astrology in 1959. The only book on the shelf was George Llewellyn's A-Z Delineator. Today there are so many books on the subject.

With such a wealth of information available the beginner can feel somewhat overwhelmed and confused about choosing an appropriate book. Just as Dorothy was guided to the first step of the yellow brick road at the beginning of her journey which changed her awareness forever, the new student of astrology may also need to be led to the text that will open that door of insight.

The Beginner's Guide to Astrological Interpretation by Joyce Levine is such a guide. I've known Joyce both professionally and personally for well over 20 years. I am delighted to see how she has grown in her own successful astrological consulting business and personally in her own awareness. In this insightful text Joyce offers students information so that they can easily digest the facts of astrology and enjoy its richness and appeal so that they are still hungry to pursue the subject in greater depth. Joyce's approach to astrology is down to earth and easy to understand so that everyone can relate to her interpretations. As you read through this book, you'll undoubtedly recognize your friends, family members, and, of course, yourself in her interpretations. It's completeness, clarity, organization, accurate information, and chart examples makes this text a wonderful initiation for the students of astrology and for teachers who are laying the foundations of astrology with their students. Even the accomplished professional can learn a thing or two.

ALPHEE LAVOIE

Introduction

This book attempts to combine the art and science of astrology. Astrology is a symbolic language, and its symbols speak to each of us differently. No two astrologers look at a chart and see exactly the same picture.

I practice astrology full time. The method of chart interpretation set forth here has been developed over the last eighteen years of seeing clients. I work to give people a better understanding of themselves and how they can best actualize their potential. I accomplish this by pointing out their natural talents and addressing their inherent stumbling blocks. My approach is psychological, and I deal with deeply rooted issues, everyday concerns, and how deeply rooted issues affect everyday concerns. I do this by approaching charts based on the way people actually live.

I know that astrologers frequently go through the chart house by house or planet by planet. For me, this doesn't make sense because life is not arranged that way. People coming in for consultations care about their families, their relationships, their careers, maybe their spiritual potential. They don't really care what the planets mean or what the aspects are. Obviously, this doesn't mean that I, as the astrologer, don't have to know these factors and consider them all. It just means I don't talk about them in this way. I give my clients what I believe helps them the most-- information in plain English.

By addressing topics such as family upbringing, relationships, and career, the consultation reflects the way people live. My orientation is very practical. I believe it's my job to interpret the planetary energies and to help my clients to understand those energies. As much as is humanly possible, I leave my own point of view out of the consultation. A right decision for me isn't necessarily correct for my clients. I let the chart tell me what I need to say.

In looking at charts, I find that all people are inconsistent by nature. There's no such thing as a "good" chart. As Scott Peck points out in The Road Less Traveled, "Life is difficult.... Once we truly know that life is difficult--once we truly understand and accept it--then life is no longer difficult." This is my approach to counseling clients. Once they recognize what they are like, including their deeply rooted stumbling blocks and those which they blame upon others, they can better deal with their lives.

I'm still struggling with how much of life is fated and how much free will we actually have. I believe a person's character is fated. She is the way she is, and there's nothing she can do about it--the chart defines this. But each person is free to live the best of her chart or the worst of it. The more I work with people, the more I believe that a human being's character does not differ a whole lot from animal instincts. A person who has an afflicted Mars gets angry or throws a temper tantrum whenever something annoys her. It's her line of least resistance. In the same way, an animal fights when it's attacked or kills food when it's hungry.

Yet, human beings have the planet Mercury, which allows them to think about their actions; and just maybe when they realize the cost of certain behavior, they can change it--although this is never easy. The difficulty of this change lies in the fact that each person views the world through his chart. Seeing it from a different view is unnatural. So, in each instance where a change would be beneficial, at the moment it should be made the person encounters tremendous resistance. Doing anything different actually seems like the wrong thing to do. A person who has a strong Saturn always feels compelled to take over responsibilities. One who has a prominent Neptune feels the need to help others and disregard the personal cost. It's only through conscious effort over a period of time that these deeply ingrained habit patterns can be changed--if then.

My work with clients is geared toward helping them recognize their paths of least resistance, which is really the whole chart, including favorable aspects. The only difference between favorable and unfavorable aspects (assuming that favorable aspects have not turned into license to do what one wants at the expense of all else) is that favorable aspects bring favorable results with ease. They are still unconsciously motivated, sometimes more so, and, because they work with so little effort, they may not be noticed as talents at all. Frequently people believe their greatest talents represent things that everyone can do because they seem so easy. So, I work with clients to take an objective view of the whole chart, of those areas which flow easily and those which need a conscious effort to change the patterns.

When I started writing this book, I intended to write a short booklet on chart interpretation. Once I started, I realized I needed to set up a common language defining signs, planets, houses, and aspects. The definitions here are not meant to be a complete examination of these factors. That would take an entire book, and many excellent ones have already been written.

While no book on interpretation can cover the same ground as would be covered during a consultation (unless a book were written on each chart), each chart analyzed here goes over the major points I would make with a client. My goal is to convey a coherent way of looking at horoscopes that approximates the way people really live.

Chapter 1

Setting Up a Context For Clients to View the Chart

Setting up a context so that clients know what to expect from a consultation is of primary importance. Few people are familiar with astrology or how it works. Even those who are aware should know the perspective of the astrologer giving the consultation, as perspectives can vary dramatically from one astrologer to another.

I start my consultations by letting a client know that his chart reflects a picture of his or her life based on his or her date, time, and place of birth.

The chart, like one's genetic programming, shows the potentials he gets to work with in life. All charts contain both favorable and difficult characteristics, so there is no such thing as a good or bad chart. The good news in this is that people are meant to be the way they are, and the bad news is that they have to live with their characteristics. Free will in this context means a person is free to live the best of his chart or the worst of it, but he cannot change the basic pattern. He is also not meant to do so, or he would have been born at another time.

A person's natural abilities, what he does well without trying, are defined by the whole chart, not just by the favorable aspects. The chart also defines problem areas. While some horoscopes seem as though they are easier to live than others, people who have what appear to be "easy" charts do not necessarily perceive their lives as easy.

The fewer tension aspects found, usually the less ability one has for dealing with tension or problems. The harder the chart the more difficult the experiences one goes through, but the better equipped he may be to handle them.

Those whose charts have a preponderance of favorable planetary relationships frequently must learn that life doesn't always go their way and that a crisis doesn't necessarily exist because they're not getting what they want at every given moment. Those whose charts have a preponderance of tense planetary relationships need to learn that they don't always have to struggle; they can find ways to handle situations more easily.

In either case, the entire horoscope tells what the beliefs are, where the beliefs come from, which are beneficial, and which produce difficulties. Each person's view is correct in some ways and flawed in others; but it can be hard to see the flaws since the chart is the lens through which one looks at life. Most people are shocked to find that the views of others differ from their own. These unexpected differences become the source of most relational conflict.

The most important point for the astrologer to remember in viewing the chart is that the whole is greater than the parts. The meaning of each component will vary from person to person because it fits into a completely different pattern. All people are inconsistent by nature, and incompatible characteristics defined by the signs, planetary combinations, or house placements do not neutralize each other. Rather, they pull people in different directions. While this is usual, it is never comfortable.

To achieve fulfillment an individual must find a way to satisfy the different sides of her nature instead of choosing one side over the other. It's up to the astrologer to point out these differing needs and help the client to recognize the importance of balancing all of them.

The astrologer in judging the horoscope should view it from the client's perspective as shown by the chart and not from her own views of life. For one client pursuing spiritual values may be the most important part of her life; for another, work or earning money; for a third relationships; for another making a mark on the world in some humanitarian, or even egoistic, way. The astrologer, as much as is humanly possible, should not impose her own values on her clients. The chart "talks to" a proficient astrologer and tells her what is important rather than the other way around.

Astrologically speaking, it's "better" to have certain placements than others; but when it comes to an individual chart, the person does not have a choice as to where his planets fall. The client doesn't benefit by hearing that Capricorn is a "bad" place for the Moon or that Mars in Pisces is disastrous. After all, this is what that person has to work with. It's the astrologer's job to help client understands what their planetary placements mean and how they can best be utilized without making value judgments about them.

The one thing the astrologer cannot tell in looking at the horoscope is the current level of individual consciousness achieved by the client. While the birth chart is the life potential, free will allows people to handle this potential differently. A difficult chart doesn't necessarily mean a doomed life or an easy chart a charmed one. It's up to each person to work out his or her potential. Some learn their "lessons" and stop repeating negative patterns. Others repeat these patterns over and over. Some develop their positive traits to their fullest capacities. Others just get by. While the chart itself gives a strong indication as to who will do what, in the end it always comes down to the individual choice of how each person handles what he's got.

Chapter 2

Defining the Signs

Understanding the positive and negative sides of each sign's character is essential for interpreting the chart. The following descriptions are particularly pertinent to the personal planets, Sun through Mars, in each sign. The placements of the outer planets, Jupiter through Pluto, because they move slowly and stay in signs for long periods of time, describe characteristics of a generation of people rather than individuals.

ARIES ♈

Aries is a cardinal, fire sign. His key words are, "I am." He rules the head. Like all fire signs, he exudes zest, enthusiasm, and spontaneity. Being the first sign of the Zodiac, he symbolizes beginnings. True to his ruler, Mars, Aries is a self-starter who courageously takes the initiative and charges forth into the unknown. He's self-centered and self-directed. Aries' competitive drive pushes him forward. He wants to be number one. Being two is like losing. But Aries competes primarily with himself. He wants to be the best he can be. He aspires to leadership positions, not so that he can tell others what to do, but so that he can do what he wants.

Aries needs less social reinforcement than other signs. As a child he lets his parents know he'd rather figure things out for himself than have their help. As an adult he's honest, direct, and straightforward. He stands up for what he believes in. Aries doesn't intend his directness to be critical or hurtful. He's not vindictive. He doesn't carry a grudge. He just says what he thinks, and he welcomes others who do the same.

Diplomacy--or sugarcoating anything--feels like dishonesty to Aries, and he makes no distinction between compromise and giving in. He finds it hard to believe that others can place more value on social approval than on doing what they think is right. This doesn't mean that he doesn't enjoy approval--although he'll never to admit that he does--but that he'll do what he believes is best despite the opinions of others. If he disagrees with what's going in a given situation and he can't change it, he'd rather go off on his own. As one Aries put it, "When I'm alone, I know I'm in good company."

Aries is quick to anger, but he is also quick to get over it. He enjoys a good argument. He has an ability for abstract thinking as well as a propensity for action, so he's equally as adept at engaging in intellectual discussions as in having an argument.

Because of Aries' tremendous energy level, he needs constant activity and accomplishes tasks faster than anyone else. To him the rest of the world moves at a frustratingly slow pace. Patience is not one of his strong points. In order to accomplish long-term goals, Aries needs to learn to wait for events to mature. While he is proficient at starting, insecurities that he keeps well hidden beneath his self-confident image emerge when events do not come to fruition quickly. His frustration can cause him to give up or do something else. This is evident in Aries' dislike of anything in which he does not immediately excel. At work he believes he should be promoted once he knows his job irrespective of the amount of time he's been there.

Romantically, this tendency manifests by Aries falling in love at first sight and hotly pursuing the object of his desire. He then easily feels rejected if the other person does not immediately return his feelings. However, once a romance matures, he needs freedom and independence--not necessarily to see another person--just to do what he wants.

TAURUS ♉

Taurus is a fixed, earth sign which gives her strong will and determination. Her key words are, "I have." She rules the throat. Like all earth signs, Taurus has a practical, material approach to life. Representing the earthy side of her ruler Venus, Taurus places a premium on comfort and security, which money and possessions help provide; but security must be emotional as well as financial. Many Taureans claim they are not interested in money, they'd rather dig in the earth--for which they enjoy a close affinity; but generally Taurus wants the soil to be found behind a large, expensive house.

Only the best will do, whether it's fine wine, a good meal, clothes that feel good as well as look good. Luxuries for now; security for later.

Taurus' desire for comfort and security can readily be seen in how she approaches new ventures. Taurus can be the hardest worker or the laziest sign of the Zodiac, depending on whether or not she considers the effort worthwhile. She proceeds cautiously into the unknown. She does not make commitments without thoroughly thinking them through. She doesn't allow herself to be pushed. Yet once she begins a project she keeps up a steady, persistent pace long after others give up.

Taurus demonstrates the earthy side of Venus in her ability to relax and enjoy herself and in her fondness for sensual delights. The taste of good food and drink, the smell of flowers or perfume, the sound of a beautiful melody, or a fond caress all appeal to Taurus. Like Cancer, she needs to be careful of becoming overweight in satisfying these delights. While Scorpio is usually considered the most sexual sign of the Zodiac, Taurus is the most sensual. While she is steadfast in relationships, she can find sensual and sexual pleasures satisfying without being tied to love.

Venus bestows Taurus with charm and grace. Others are attracted to what appears to be her easy-going manner. While Taurus dislikes fights and arguments and avoids them whenever possible, she's a fixed sign who can be stubborn and obstinate. She's determined to get her way no matter how charmingly she handles situations. Just because she doesn't argue, one cannot assume she has given in. Taurus' unspoken motto is, "Let's not fight about it, let's just do it my way." She doesn't lose her temper often, but watch out when she does.

Taurus proceeds slowly in committing to relationships, but is loyal, protective, and dependable once she does. She places a strong value on home and family--and she wants her home to be her castle. She knows how to cook, loves gardening; and as a spouse or parent, she gives nurturance and protection to her loved ones. She's the most emotionally sensitive of the earth signs, but she has to be wary of being overly possessive. At her worst, she can treat those she loves like possessions, with a "this is mine" attitude.

GEMINI Ⅱ

Gemini is a mutable, air sign. He rules the nervous system, hands, shoulders, arms, lungs. His key words are, "I think." And true to his ruler Mercury, think he does. Like all air signs, Gemini wants life to have logical A + B = C explanations. He forever questions why things are the way they are and does not trust what cannot be explained. His own intellect is keen and decisive, even if his actions are not always so.

Gemini's natural skills make him a good writer, teacher, reporter, sales person, or public relations expert. He excels in any field involving communication so long as it has variety. He also excels at working with his hands. Talented and versatile, Gemini can't stand routine. He's better at performing five tasks at a time than at sitting down with one until it's completed. If he cannot have variety, he's best at coming up with the ideas and letting others carry them out.

Gemini is happy as long as he is learning. Intellectual challenge stimulates him. On the job, once there's nothing left to learn he becomes bored and yearns for something else, regardless of the financial remuneration.

Gemini's sharp mind and wit and good sense of humor make him fun to be around. He enjoys meeting and socializing with different types of people, but he's actually more interested in their ideas than in the people themselves. This accounts for his restlessness--and his bad reputation. Since he becomes so engrossed in conversation, his interest appears to be in the person with whom he's conversing. This can make it look as though he's flirting when that's the last thing on his mind. And when he no longer finds interesting those with whom he's conversing, he moves on to the next conversation, accounting for his reputation for fickleness.

Gemini needs intellectual companionship in all relationships. While he would hate to admit it, he can be an intellectual snob. Romantically, having someone he can talk to is far more important than having a dynamic sexual relationship. Gemini also needs the illusion of freedom in his romances. He hates the thought of being fenced in. He needs to believe he can come and go as he pleases; but if he's allowed to do so, he may not necessarily go anywhere.

This is not to say that Gemini does not have a changeable nature, because he does. What he says today may not be what he means tomorrow. Flexible in his thinking and forever learning, he's always willing to change his mind--even when this conflicts with commitments he's already made. In relationships this can manifest with his making a quick exit when things are not going the way he thinks they should be. While Gemini relishes intellectual arguments where he can talk others into his ideas and then take the other side of an issue to test his persuasiveness, he behaves very differently when it comes to serious disagreements. He'd rather switch than fight--or pretend to switch to avoid obstacles or conflict. In a serious disagreement, it's hard to get a straight answer from him.

CANCER ♋

Cancer is a cardinal, water sign. Her key words are, "I feel." Cancer rules the chest, breasts, and the stomach. True to her ruler, the Moon, Cancer derives information from the world around her through her instincts and feelings. She cannot explain how she knows, she just does. Also, since her ruler, the Moon, is the repository of memories, Cancer vividly remembers the past. She retains strong family bonds regardless of the ease or difficulty of the relationships or geographical distance.

Whether a male or female, Cancer represents the mother of the Zodiac. She protects, sustains, and nurtures. She's sensitive to the needs of others as well to her own. Home and family come first. She takes care of her aging parents as she would her children. At her best, she extends the protectiveness of a family environment to friends, co-workers, social organizations, town, country.

Her ability to perceive what's going on beneath the surface, what's unspoken, manifests in her lending a helping hand to others without their having to ask. She shows up with chicken soup for a sick friend or makes sure co-workers have a place to go for holiday dinners.

The unspoken deal Cancer makes with Significant Others is, "You take care of me, and I'll take care of you." At her worst, she portrays the mother figure who manipulates those around her with guilt when they do not comply with her spoken or unspoken demands. She can also be amazingly insensitive to the plight of those not in her "group."

While Cancer is sensitive to even the most constructive criticism, her reputation for timidity is much overrated. It comes from her dislike of starting anything until she knows how it will end. If she's on step one and she doesn't know how step ten will turn out, she feels insecure and has difficulty taking action. This leads her to procrastinate, but in familiar situations, Cancer initiates without difficulty.

Cancer, like Taurus, values security, financial and emotional, above all else. She worries about the future. She must have money saved for a rainy day-- which she never expects to spend. When it comes to romance, she wants assurances that she will be loved forever before she consents to get involved. On becoming a parent, she has to take care that her concern for her children's safety does not interfere with her relationship with her spouse.

Obviously, not all Cancers are women who stay home with children. Those in the work place are motivated by the desire to provide security for themselves and their families.

Cancer hates disagreements. She sidesteps direct conflict like the crab retreating into its shell, but she displays expertise in passive resistance. She can retreat to food for comfort when upset. And even when she's not upset, she has to be careful of gaining weight easily and retaining water.

While Cancer's curiosity pries secrets out of others, she keeps hers hidden, along with the mementos that she saves for their sentimental value. Scorpio is usually considered the most secretive sign of the Zodiac, but Cancer has her beat. While Scorpio does not tell others what she does not want to, Cancer purposely goes out of her way to hide what she considers personal.

LEO ♌

Leo is a fixed, fire sign. He rules the heart, spine, and back. His key words are, "I will." Like all fire signs, he displays zest, enthusiasm, and spontaneity. And like his ruler, the Sun, which shines in the heavens, Leo's motto is, "I have to be me." Self-expression is a necessity for this generous and noble sign. He must love whatever he does to feel alive.

As a fixed sign, once Leo makes a commitment, personally or professionally, he follows through faithfully. He's persistent, well organized, and finishes what he starts. He wants to be the authority figure and functions well in positions of responsibility or management, but he doesn't do as well in subservient roles. Leo hates to be told what to do or how to do it. It offends his dignity. He must learn how to take orders until it's his turn to be at the top.

Dramatically expressive, Leo enjoys the limelight. Like an actor with star quality, he seems to say, "I'm wonderful." But the question underneath it is, "Aren't I?" Leo needs the reinforcement of being looked up to, admired, and respected, but he wants to be admired for himself. He will courageously take an unpopular stand if he believes it to be the right one. He's honest and direct and will not pretend to be something he's not in order to win approval. He expects that same honesty in return. This is the naiveté of fire signs--because they are direct and honest, they assume others will be also.

Male or female, Leo considers his appearance no small matter. Like Libra, he always makes sure he looks his best. But unlike Libra, Leo has a flair for dramatics, whether it be in the way he dresses, the lavish parties he loves to throw, or the way he embellishes the stories he tells.

Leo is the fire sign most concerned with people. In all relationships, Leo displays loyalty and faithfulness. As a parent, he's protective. In intimate relationships, he's affectionate and loving and wants affection displayed in return. When he's appreciated, there is nothing he will not do for others. On the other hand, he never forgets an offense to his pride. Feeling appreciated can present a problem for Leo. At his worst, no matter how much attention he gets, he still craves more. Not prone to introspection and being self-centered, he can forget that everyone else's life does not necessarily revolve around him.

Straightening out relational problems is not easy for Leo. At his worst, he'd rather walk away with his pride than risk rejection. He can be more concerned with how he appears than with getting what he wants. This also influences what he goes after. Although Leo will take risks when he's confident, he's capable of avoiding situations where he may not look good--no matter how much he desires the results.

VIRGO ♍

Virgo is a mutable, earth sign. She rules the intestines and the spleen. Her key words, "I analyze," symbolize the combination of her ruler, Mercury, with the element of earth. This combination gives her a sharp intellect and common sense. She's not interested in ideas for themselves, but in what can be done with them.

Virgo represents the worker who perfects her craft whatever it may be. She accomplishes tasks in a practical, methodical, and detailed manner while maintaining a flexible attitude. She is always willing to make changes if someone shows her a more efficient way to produce results. She reliably performs her duties in the "right way," no matter what the pay. This makes Virgo the least materialistic of the earth signs.

Because her discriminating intellect naturally breaks things down into their component parts, she learns easily from how-to manuals and can excel at writing them as well as in teaching and training others. Virgo also excels in working with her hands.

Virgo always wants to improve. She continues learning long after her formal education concludes. She emulates an ideal of detail perfection. Her checkbook must be balanced, her work space neat, her home clean. At the same time she tries to improve the world and the people around her. This gives rise to her reputation for being critical. Since self-improvement is so important to her, she finds it hard to believe that others do not fervently embrace this goal. At her worst, she's a terrible nag who points out the flaws of others for their "own good." Virgo needs to learn when suggestions are helpful and when they are just plain criticism.

Virgo's never-ending desire to improve herself contributes to her lack of self-confidence. She can be so wrapped up in her flaws that she has a hard time believing that others mean it when they compliment her. As no one ever achieves perfection, Virgo frequently believes she's not good enough. Her tendency to worry about the little things actually hampers her performance and at her worst can cause her to miss the big picture. This is seen in the work place by her tendency to put time into details that others do not value, which can in turn lead to her being criticized for not producing enough despite her hard work. When in a position of authority, she has difficulty delegating work for fear than no one else will do it well enough. Even when she's succeeding she has to watch the tendency not to apply for promotions until she's thinks that she's attained perfection in her current position.

In romance Virgo also carefully discriminates. A single Virgo has been known to dismiss a suitor if his shoes were not shined or if his nail were not manicured. No matter how hard Virgo falls in love, she can still objectively list her lover's good and bad traits. Aside from herself, she's the most critical of those she loves the best--who else would she rather help? Virgo shows her feelings for others by doing something tangible to take care of them. Love for her comes from what one does, not from what one says.

While Virgo's modesty easily fits her association with the virgin symbology, she's still an earth sign who enjoys physical pleasure.

LIBRA ♎

Libra is a cardinal, air sign. His key words are "I balance." He rules the kidneys. His ruler, Venus, conveys charm and grace upon him as well as an eye for beauty. As the sign of marriage, relationships, and partnership, Libra values harmony and cooperation above all else. He seeks balance and moderation, carefully weighing all sides of an issue before coming to a conclusion. He dislikes arguments and crude behavior. He believes it's important to get along well with others, and he cares what they think of him.

Libra's moderate, "peace at any price" nature can cause others to underestimate him. He's a logical, intellectual sign that needs mental stimulation. He works equally as well with systems and ideas as with people. Libra excels at diplomacy. And like diplomats, he often gets people to do what he wants while they believe it is they who came up with the ideas. This ability to bring others over to his side without conflict makes Libra a good lawyer, executive, or counselor. Being stronger willed than others anticipate, Libra earns his reputation for wearing a velvet glove over an iron fist.

This velvet glove shows in his dislike of crass behavior. Libra, the master of social appropriateness, believes people should be "nice." That's why he doesn't like to fight. It's also why, at his worst, it's so difficult to get a straight answer from him. He's capable of telling others what they want to hear regardless of what he really thinks. Yet, his reputation for indecisiveness is overrated. It stems from his tendency to look for a way to "have it all" himself and please everybody else at the same time.

To Libra, life without a Significant Other-- whether it's a spouse, lover, or best friend--is unimaginable. He wants to someone to share his life with, someone whom he considers an equal and who shares his interests and ideas, or the relationship has no meaning. Because of this, Libra may be expected to be emotional; but like all air signs, he relates mind to mind and is much more comfortable thinking than feeling. This contributes to his tendency to rationalize remaining in unsuitable relationships. While Libra can manage by himself perfectly well, at his most self-destructive, he avoids being alone no matter what the circumstances. One Libra, upon being asked for a divorce during a Neptune transit, commented "I never expected it. We weren't fighting." The fact that he and his wife had not spoken to each other in years had slipped his mind.

Another side of Libra's velvet glove gets expressed through Libra's esthetic sense. He appreciates culture and enjoys art, theater, and music. He dresses well and likes to be noticed. Female Libras frequently adorn themselves with decorative jewelry, usually made out of copper (ruled by Venus) and semi- precious stones. Compliments go a long way toward winning Libra's heart.

SCORPIO ♏

Scorpio is a fixed, water sign. She rules the sex organs. Her key words are "I create." Despite her calm exterior that appears to be unemotional, Scorpio is an intensely emotional sign which lives by passion. She takes an all or nothing approach to whatever she does. She makes no distinction between moderation and apathy. Her passion is frequently misunderstood as purely sexual, but it's a passion for life. Scorpio is either in love or not interested, whether it's with a person, a job, or an idea.

This makes Scorpio, like her ruler Pluto, capable of achieving great heights or sinking into the depths. She is the only sign that has more than one symbol. At her lowest level, she displays the famous qualities of the arachnid with the poisonous sting. This sting can be seen when she's hurt or in a bad mood, and her piercing tongue cuts others to the quick as she contemplates revenge. At her highest level, she's the Phoenix who rose out of the ashes, symbolizing resurrection and transformation. No matter where Scorpio is in her life, or how much she has accomplished, she's always trying to transcend, to be better. In the middle, she's the eagle who flies higher than any other bird, but can still descend to the depths. Scorpio's challenge is to chose among them.

The natural psychologist of the Zodiac, Scorpio has good instincts about people and situations. She intuitively pierces through things, getting right to the core of their underlying meaning, irrespective of whether she's analyzing a person, a procedure, or an ideal, or whether she's looking for the meaning of life--which she fully expects to find.

Because her instincts are so good, Scorpio bases her decisions entirely on how she feels--no matter how pragmatic her justifications for them may sound. She then puts a tremendous amount of will power into achieving what she desires. The problem is that she's so sure she's right, she doesn't stop to reexamine her choices. If she's headed in the right direction, her determination and sheer will get her favorable results. If she's headed in the wrong direction, she still gets results, but not those she bargained for.

Some say that Scorpio tries to control her environment because she cannot, or does not wish to, control herself. Whatever the case, she needs to learn not to make her desires more important than she is. When she wants something, she can forget that she's the one who chose it. Her feelings are so tied into her desires that accomplishing whatever she wants can feel like a life or death issue--"My life is over if this doesn't work out." She also needs to learn that it's possible for her--like anyone else--to make a mistake, and that just because she wants something doesn't always mean it's right for her.

In romantic relationships, this can be seen by her staying in unhappy relationships for a long time, all the while trying to "fix up" her lover so that they can both be happy. Her passion can definitely cloud her judgment. Her reputation as a sex symbol is much overrated, but love for Scorpio does require passion. There's never too much sex with the right person, but she won't let the wrong one, i.e., someone she's not attracted to, hold her hand. At her worst, Scorpio can be jealous, possessive, and controlling. Scorpio's romantic lesson is to distinguish passion and chemistry from love.

In all relationships, Scorpio is vehemently loyal and trustworthy. She gives a lot, and expects a lot in return. While there is nothing she will not do for those she cares about, she still expects them to be self-sufficient. And, like Virgo, she's always looking to improve herself and finds it hard to believe when others do not feel the same way.

SAGITTARIUS ♐

Sagittarius is a mutable, fire sign. He rules the hips, thighs, and liver. His key words are "I perceive." Sagittarius wants life to be an adventure, chock-full of travel and excitement. He values freedom and independence above all else, whether it's freedom of action or freedom of mind. He's talkative, friendly, outgoing, and fun to be around, so he effortlessly charms others, but he does his own thing and will not be fenced in.

Like his fellow fire sign Aries, he's direct and honest. He says whatever is on his mind in no uncertain terms and can be surprised when this hurts the feelings of others. Truth--at least his impression of it--is more important to him than tact and diplomacy, and it is difficult for him to imagine that others do not think the same way. True to his ruler, Jupiter, he's optimistic and positive thinking, regardless of his current circumstances. Gambling and risk-taking come naturally to him because he expects to be lucky. His faith in the future can carry him through the most difficult of times; or at his worst, it can bring him into difficult times because of his "why do anything; life will take care of me" attitude.

Sagittarius is the most intellectual of the fire signs. He's concerned with ideas and ideals, whether the ideas are philosophical, religious, or just beliefs about how people should live. He can stand up for social reform on one hand or be a spokesperson for the prevailing social order on the other. Although he can proselytize an ideal, his involvement remains intellectual rather than action-oriented. He's concerned with theoretical concepts, not with mundanely working out those concepts. Being a mutable sign, he's also not afraid to change his mind. While he can argue fervently for an ideal, if he later decides he was on the wrong side of the issue, he can publicly argue just as fervently for the opposing view. Either way, he must be careful of being prejudiced against those who do not believe in his system of thought.

There are two types of Sagittarius. One is the philosophical, scholarly type who's concerned with learning and gaining wisdom. He wants to improve the social order in which he lives. Still his contribution remains intellectual, not pragmatic. He makes a good minister or humanitarian worker, but his interest is in society, not the individual.

The other type of Sagittarius is more concerned for himself. His sense of freedom takes precedence above all else. His desire for travel, excitement, and adventure can outweigh his willingness to deal with the responsibilities of everyday life. He promises, with the best of intentions, more than he delivers. Optimistically, he believes he'll come through, but he doesn't worry much about it when he does not. One person can play both Sagittarius roles in a lifetime.

Both types enjoy the outdoors. Hiking, horseback riding, communing with nature gives Sagittarius a sense of tranquillity not likely to be found elsewhere.

CAPRICORN ♑

Capricorn is a cardinal, earth sign. She rules the knees, skin, and bones. Her key words are "I use." Like all earth signs, Capricorn approaches life from a practical, material viewpoint. Before she believes anything, she needs to see the tangible proof. She's not interested in abstract ideas; instead she wants to know how they will work. As an earth sign, Capricorn is a feminine sign. This femininity is expressed by her accepting societal rules of right and wrong, but there's nothing receptive in the way that Capricorn goes after what she wants.

True to her ruler Saturn, Capricorn is born mature, serious, and responsible. She is old from an early age and has a strong sense of duty. She does the right thing because it's the thing to do. As a child, Capricorn takes out the garbage and helps around the house because the chores need to get done. Childhood may not be particularly fun for her; she oftentimes gets along better with adults than with children her own age. She's too little to play with the big kids and those her age seem too immature. Her life gets easier as she gets older because at some point her age catches up with her maturity.

Capricorn's seriousness does not diminish as an adult. She's patient, persistent, and a good organizer. Her discipline and a strong sense of purpose endow her with a capacity for hard work. She puts in the time and effort it takes to get ahead. In performing tasks she looks to see how they were traditionally handled and improves upon the standard methods. She plays by the rules of whatever environment she's in. She respects authority because ultimately she expects to be the authority figure. Status, position, power, being looked up to and respected, mean a great deal to her. Capricorn wants to be the boss, to have the power to call the shots; she's executive material and wants to be recognized as such. Position is as important, if not more so, than money.

Obviously, not every Capricorn becomes a CEO, although they would all certainly like to be.

For Capricorn to have a sense of achievement in the work arena, she must be in charge of whatever she's doing and be the authority in that domain, no matter how large or small.

Capricorn has an unlikely naiveté stemming from her belief that those who do what is considered "the right thing" will be rewarded for their effort. Unfortunately, the fact that life does not always turn out so fairly can lead Capricorn to despair.

Capricorn's social and political views are conservative. She believes people deserve what they work for, no more, no less. Yet, at the same time, she's always there to help those who rely on her. In all relationships, she has to learn when not to take over or try to fix up the problems of others. Her sense of duty and obligation make it hard for her to say no when they call upon her.

Capricorn is not comfortable with feelings. Emotional expression does not come easily so she can appear cold or as if she doesn't care about people. In her youth she must be careful that she does not sacrifice human relationships in her quest for status and success. It's easier for her to handle tasks than to express feelings. Even at her best, she's more likely to do something for those she cares about than talk about how she feels. At her worst, this can cause her to withdraw from relationships, feeling rejected when others do not appreciate her efforts to take care of them or when they do not take care of her in a reciprocal manner. Capricorn counts--"I did this for you. What did you do for me?"

Capricorn is not usually considered the sexiest of signs. However, Capricorn women such as Ava Gardner frequently play the role of femme fatales. And while Capricorns are not affectionately demonstrative in public--it's bad taste--they are an earth sign, so what's done in private is another matter.

Finally, Capricorn is the only sign which gets younger as she gets older. As she becomes more successful, she allows herself to enjoy life in a way that was not possible during her younger years when achievement came first.

AQUARIUS ≈

Aquarius is a fixed air sign. His key words are "I know." He rules the ankles and circulatory system. He's associated with friendship, group activities, and at his highest level, the brotherhood of man, symbolized by the water bearer spilling out life force and spiritual energy.

Like all air signs, Aquarius faces life through his intellect, but through his Uranian rulership ideas come to him in moments of inspiration that appear like a lightning flash. He's a mental pioneer, who's individualistic, creative, and inventive. His interests lie in anything new, different, and out of the ordinary--whether it's people, places, or ideas. He doesn't care about the past or tradition. Aquarius believes in breaking down boundaries and moving into new territory.

Aquarius is friendly and outgoing. He enjoys meeting people and easily fits into new social surroundings. He values friendship and exchange of ideas with a wide variety of people. He has many friends--and he counts acquaintances as friends--for his different interests. He accepts people for the way they are, and the more unusual they are, the better he likes them. But he has two prejudices. He can't stand stupid people, which he differentiates from unlearned; and he can't stand conservatives.

Yet Aquarius himself is hard to get to know. He relates to people through his intellect, not through his feelings, which he has trouble admitting he has. (Everyone has a Moon.) He views the world from a detached perspective that borders on coldness and can't understand when others don't do the same. As long as he's being honest, he doesn't think his behavior should upset anyone. A female Aquarius, upon asking her lover to move out of their apartment, couldn't understand why he was upset when she started seeing other men before he had left. She had been honest with him; what more did he want? He, being a Taurus, had a very different perspective.

It's easier for Aquarius to have relationships with groups of people than to relate to one person. In love affairs, as in the rest of his life, he does not want to be fenced in. His freedom means more to him than any person, and a lasting relationship must be based upon freedom of choice and separate identities. Also, Aquarius will not give up his friends, including those of the opposite sex, for a lover. As an air sign, he does not see sex as a primary concern; but he does believe sex to be a natural extension of friendship, so lovers can become friends; friends can become lovers with or without a romantic attachment.

Aquarius' liberal ideas make him appear open minded and easy going, but he's a fixed sign who's stubborn about his ideas and his belief system. On one hand, Aquarius is a humanitarian. He swears by freedom and individual liberty for all. On the other hand, once he adopts a belief system, he's so convinced of its truth that he wants everyone else to believe it too. His loyalties to his group, where he usually can be found in a leadership position, can be so strong that he dismisses all those who disagree with its philosophy, all the while preaching freedom of thought and liberty. He may love mankind, but he has difficulties with individuals.

PISCES ♓

Pisces is a mutable water sign. Her key words are "I believe." She rules the feet and the lymphatic system. Pisces is the most sensitive, imaginative, and compassionate sign of the Zodiac. She is also creative, psychic, and spiritually oriented.

Like all water signs, Pisces lives in her feelings. But water signs express their sensitivities differently. Cancer's primary concern is for her family, Scorpio's for whomever she chooses to care about, while Pisces' sensitivity extends to everyone and everything. She can read a sad story in the paper and be upset. Situations don't have to happen to her or her friends, relatives, or neighbors for her to be emotionally concerned.

Like her ruler, Neptune, Pisces lacks boundaries. Her sensitivity causes her to absorb unconsciously what's going on around her. She has difficulty distinguishing her own feelings from the vibrations of her environment. If she's upset and her environment is jovial, her mood will improve. If she is happy and the environment is sad, she takes on its sadness. Because of this she needs time to retreat and to be alone. Through meditation she can learn to distinguish what stems from herself and what comes from the environment.

Pisces has a poetic soul, strong imagination, and creative vision. She's the most artistic of all the signs. She more than loves what's beautiful; she feels connected with it. Creative endeavors such as poetry, art, music, dance, and theater whether for fun or for profit, provide healthy escapes for her. If she's sad or upset, listening to beautiful music or taking a trip to a museum can put her in a better mood.

Pisces is a romantic idealist who longs to transcend earthly existence. She sees life the way it should be. She sees the best in people and situations. Her attitude is, "Why see the bad when you can see the good?" In romance Pisces wants to fall in love with Prince (or Princess) Charming and live happily ever after. She puts her lover on a pedestal. She becomes an actress and plays whatever part she believes he would like--after all, he's so wonderful how could she help herself? The problem is that she's longing for a romantic ideal, a union with God, and that longing is unlikely to be satisfied by a mere human being.

Her idealism and sensitivity, coupled with her strong sympathy for the underdog, cause her to take care of others, regardless of the romantic attachment. She has difficulty saying no, refusing another whose need may be greater than her own. Idealistically, this appears very noble, but in real life it causes her tremendous pain. Pisces unwillingness to see people's flaws makes her a poor judge of character. She has a way of choosing people who will take advantage of her, and the faults she refuses to see have a way of hitting her over the head when she least expects it. The difference between the way life is supposed to be and the way it is becomes her nemesis. She feels crushed when she discovers that she's been deceived, regardless of whether she was purposely deceived by the other person or by her image of him.

When disappointed, Pisces seeks to escape. At best, she needs time alone. At worst, she falls prey to drugs and alcohol. Given her physically sensitive system and her dislike of the material world, if she falls too far, it can be difficult to climb out.

There's a negative side of Pisces that's rarely discussed. It happens when her sensitivities turn inward instead of outward. She still cares for those around her, but she becomes too immersed in her own feelings to be concerned for anyone else. She expresses an "I'm feeling bad, take care of me" attitude and becomes demanding.

Pisces' main lesson in life comes from the discrepancies between the spiritual ideal and the real in the physical universe. While her ruler Neptune's view of transcendence, love, and peace predominate on the spiritual plane, those on earth still live under Saturn's domain and must pay at least some homage to his rule.

Chapter 3

Planets

The following describes the planets as they are found in the natal chart. Transiting planets do not always assume the same functions.

The Sun through Mars are personal planets. The signs they fall in directly affect a person's sense of identity. Jupiter through Pluto are outer planets. Because they move slowly, the signs they fall in define the times one is born into. Uranus through Pluto, particularly, are more important for an individual by house position and aspect than by sign.

SUN ☉

The Sun represents one's basic sense of identity. A person asked to describe himself is likely to list his Sun sign characteristics. The Sun represents one's will, power, creative expression, individuation, and constitutional strength. Its energy is masculine. It rules the heart and the spine.

Positive expression of the Sun endows inner strength, power, courage, and confidence. Negative expression becomes willfulness, arrogance, and egocentricity.

Favorable aspects to the Sun from any planet assist a person in expressing his individuality along the lines of the planetary influence. Unfavorable aspects thwart an individual or compel him to act in accordance with the aspecting planet's influence. A heavily aspected Sun--regardless of the aspects--endows a great deal of drive and power of self-expression.

MOON ☽

The Moon shows the emotional nature, how one mothers or takes care of others, the emotional impact of the family, and the emotional impact of past and present experiences. Its energy is feminine. The Moon rules the stomach and breasts, all sacks or containers in the body, and, together with Venus, the female organs.

The Moon positively expressed is sensitivity, nurturance, and protectiveness to others as well as oneself. The Moon negatively expressed includes mood swings for no apparent reason, emotional instability, and possessiveness under the guise of being protective.

A person with a favorably aspected Moon allows herself to feel, regardless of what those feelings are. A person with an unfavorably aspected Moon experiences stifled or exaggerated feelings in accordance with its planetary aspects.

MERCURY ☿

Mercury tells how one thinks, communicates, and learns. It represents logic and reasoning. It rules the nervous system. Mercury is neither a masculine nor feminine planet. Its androgynous energy is colored by the sign it falls in. Its sign and house positions and aspects determine what information a person pays attention to. The importance of this cannot be overrated. How a person focuses his thoughts and the way in which he interprets information forms the basis for his future actions.

Favorable aspects to Mercury enhance one's ability to learn and communicate and to objectively interpret the world around him. Unfavorable aspects form obstacles to rational decision making in accordance with the planet making the aspect. For instance, Mercury difficultly aspected to Saturn conveys negative thinking, a worrier who looks for what can go wrong. This can in turn adversely affect a person's ability to take action. Obviously, the rest of the chart must be taken into consideration in this determination.

While Mercury's positive expression conveys a keen intellect, the ability to analyze, and mental agility, Mercury's negative expression is indecisiveness, verbosity, and coldness when the intellect rules above all else.

VENUS ♀

Venus shows the person's ideal of love and beauty, how she gives love and wants to receive it (including sexually), her social adeptness, and her sense of worth in relationships. Venus' nature is feminine and represents the power of attraction. Venus rules venous blood, the throat, the larynx, the kidneys, and the female organs.

Venus, through her Taurus rulership, is frequently associated with a person's money-making capability, but Venus does not directly relate to one's income unless she falls in the second, sixth, or tenth houses. However, a favorably aspected Venus draws opportunities to her by her sociability. When Venus is favorably aspected, a person feels desirable and worthy of love and can easily relate to others. When Venus is afflicted, she does not feel her own worth, which results in relational problems in line with the afflicting planet.

Venus positively expressed seeks harmony and affection. Negatively expressed Venus conveys indolence: Why do anything? My beauty will get me through; and superficiality: I'm as nice as I pretend to be.

For both males and females, Venus and the Moon represent the feminine archetype: what ones wants in a relationship, how he or she feels about it, and how he or she takes care of or nurtures others. For a man, these planets represent his ideal image of a woman. For a female, they represent the roles she plays. For a male these planets also represent his relational roles, but he will not be conscious of this unless he has incorporated his anima into his own consciousness. Otherwise he will expect the woman in his life to act out these roles and be disappointed if and when this does not happen.

MARS ♂

Mars shows one's energy, drive and initiative, how he goes after what he wants, how he expresses force, strength, and courage or anger and temper and sexual desire. Mars emphasizes individual action and separateness. It is a masculine planet that rules the muscular system and the head.

Favorable aspects to Mars assist a person in taking the necessary action to achieve his goals. Unfavorable aspects hinder this action and give rise to a bad temper along the lines of the planet making the aspect.

Mars' positive expression is enthusiasm, spontaneity, dynamic action, and courage. Its negative expression is violence, cruelty, and domination, fighting for the sake of the fight rather than the cause, or "Get out of my way, I'm getting what I want."

The **combination of the Sun and Mars** shows the masculine archetype found in the chart for both men and women. They represent the sense of identity as described by the Sun, its sign, house placement, and aspects, and how one goes about manifesting that identity as described by Mars, its sign, house placement, and aspects. The chart as a whole obviously contributes to this picture. For women, the Sun and Mars represent her ideal male image. Women today seem better able to own these planets as their own energy than men seem to do with the feminine counterparts of Venus and the Moon.

For both sexes **Mars and Venus** represent the sexual couple. Mars plays the role of aggressor; Venus plays the part of attraction. Both sexes play both roles.

JUPITER ♃

Jupiter represents the expansion principle, luck or ease, prosperity, and optimism. It also represents one's values whether expressed through philosophy or religious beliefs or attitudes toward day-to-day life. As Jupiter has a twelve-year cycle, everyone born within a year has Jupiter in the same sign. Whether its values are integrated into the person's life or are ideals that are never acted out depends upon planetary aspects to Jupiter. It rules the liver and the veins.

The positive side of Jupiter, usually expressed through favorable aspects, embodies idealism, philanthropy, faith, generosity, and luck.

The negative side, usually expressed through difficult aspects, conveys extravagance and indulgence. People with harsh Jupiter configurations expect the same luck that easy configurations convey, but they do not get it. At their worst, those with a strong Jupiter can believe the world owes them a living.

Adverse aspects to Jupiter can also endow the bigoted with the belief that everyone should buy into their particular belief system. Religious wars, such as the Crusades, were Jupiterian as well as Martian. In today's world with the advent of atomic energy, there is the danger of religious wars becoming Plutonian as well as Jupiterian.

SATURN ♄

Saturn represents the reality structure on the earth plane. It makes the rules, sets the limits, and defines the structure. In this way Saturn represents the work ethic, responsibility, organization, the rules or "shoulds" one must live up to. It also rules time, which may be the greatest limitation, delay, and old age. Saturn creates boundaries which can provide safety and protection or which can be limiting and inhibiting. Saturn rules the bones, skin, and teeth.

The positive side of Saturn comes forth when one realistically assesses himself and the world around him (realistically does not mean negatively); when, with common sense and discipline, he lives up to his responsibilities, and, ultimately, when he learns from his experiences.

Saturn, negatively expressed, still acts responsibly. The difference is that responsibility becomes burden and that one becomes responsible at the expense of himself, rather than responsibility enhancing his life. This can cause a person to have a low self- worth and to be fearful, pessimistic, and exacting.

Those with a favorably aspected Saturn assume responsibilities easily, but know how to set limits that benefit them.

Those with Saturn negatively aspected, particularly to the inner planets, believe that they're not good enough unless they live up to the expectations of others, even though these expectations are more likely to be their own than anyone else's. They have difficulties with authority figures. They see barriers where none may exist and easily feel rejected.

These issues are handled in two very different ways. Either people push through their barriers to achievement to prove they're good enough, or they retreat when they come up to these barriers because they don't believe they can break through them.

A person with a strong, difficultly aspected Saturn needs to learn that he's not answerable for everyone else's life and what goes on in it and that truly being responsible means being responsible to oneself and one's own needs first, not as license, but as self-nurturance and self-acceptance.

URANUS ♅

Uranus represents freedom, independence, individuality, originality, and enlightenment through a lightning flash, a sudden burst of inspiration. It rules fields of study that are mind-oriented such as science, computer technology, and astrology. Its energy is disruptive and unexpected. It rules the nervous system.

Uranus' positive urgings help one to break through his barriers (Saturn creations) and push him toward being himself. They display resourcefulness and a pioneering spirit. In a societal context these urgings challenge the social structure and help create new realities that are more just than those they destroy.

Uranus' negative urgings incite a person to be free at the expense of being responsible and cause him to flaunt disruptive behavior. They bring forth radicalness, eccentricity, and a cold detachment. Stalinist-like revolutions represent Uranus' negative manifestation in the social order, destroying the opposition by literally killing them off.

In these instances, the true meaning of freedom is subverted. Freedom becomes "freedom from" rather than the "freedom to be oneself." A rebellious "I don't have to do what you want" supersedes the natural sense of "I have to be me."

Since Uranus is in a sign for seven years, it, along with Neptune and Pluto, shows the Zeitgeist of the generation in which one is born. Uranus' house placement and aspects are more important than its sign on a personal level.

A favorably aspected Uranus allows one to be oneself without conflict and to naturally express a courageous spirit. A person with a negatively aspected Uranus tends to rebel against authority, confusing freedom with rebellion and throwing it in the face of others, no matter what the circumstances are or what the consequences may be.

NEPTUNE Ψ

Neptune rules sympathy and compassion, and universal love and beauty. It also rules psychic ability, dreams, spirituality, and the astral plane. Its negative manifestations include all escapist behavior, drugs, alcohol, illusion, and victimization.

Neptune remains in a sign for fourteen years so that its sign position, like that of Uranus and Pluto, emphasizes the cultural values at the time of one's birth. Neptune actually represents the cultural ideals. For instance, when Neptune falls in Capricorn, conservative ideas, big business, money, and the work ethic become the ideals of the time. By contrast, the previous fourteen years when Neptune transited Sagittarius, the ideals were a shorter work week, more leisure time, and increased travel. Neptune's house position and aspects play a more important role for an individual than its sign.

Neptune rules Heaven and its ideals are the way the world would be if everything were perfect. However, those ideals don't work well on the physical plane until one is grounded in Saturn's reality. If Neptune is more strongly placed than Saturn, a quest for spirituality and the longing for a Heaven-like existence can actually be nothing more

046

than the desire to escape from the demands of everyday life.

Neptune's positive side urges universal love, caring, and understanding. While favorable aspects to it are more likely to bring about its positive manifestation, with Neptune there is no guarantee. When it is strongly emphasized, both favorable and unfavorable aspects can cause illusion, because one wants to see what's beautiful and not what's unpleasant, even when this means tuning out the not-so-beautiful realities that must be dealt with in everyday life. Its planetary energy is difficult to handle because it creates blind spots, and one cannot handle what one cannot see.

PLUTO ♇

Pluto rules inner drive or compulsion, power of will, focused attention, the urge for deep understanding and change or transformation, and desires including, but not limited to sex. It is associated with death and resurrection. Pluto's energy stems from deep within the unconscious. It rules the sex organs. A highly emphasized Pluto in the birth chart conveys mighty power for good or evil. It's exceptionally magnetic energy either strongly attracts or repels.

The positive expression of Pluto takes form as concentrated effort. It urges one to understand through knowledge, to seek wisdom, to change and transform. This may take place on a personal level or a societal level. Pluto rules healers, therapists, politicians, and religious leaders.

The negative expression of Pluto includes death, annihilation, obsession, and the destructive side of power and control. Dictators, organized crime, gangs, atomic weapons, and twentieth century wars where complete annihilation is possible fall under Pluto's domain.

On a personal level, its power can manifest by a person's exerting stringent control over his environment because he cannot control himself. On a psychological level, a person is actually dependent upon what he desires to control, but his use of power covers up this dependency.

Mythologically, Pluto was the god of the underworld. Its reputation comes mostly through the myth of Persephone rather than direct knowledge about the planet itself. In the birth chart, Pluto operates much the same way. It's easier to understand Pluto through the aspects it makes to other planets. Pluto intensifies their natural tendencies. When Pluto aspects Venus natally, love becomes deep but also compulsive.

Easy aspects to Pluto make it easier for an individual to harness and utilize its power without experiencing inner turmoil. He still has strong desires, but they seem easier to satisfy. Also, he can better manipulate others because his need to control is not apparent.

Harsh aspects from Pluto form strong compulsions expressed through the aspected planet. These aspects give one the feeling that if the desire does not get satisfied, his life will be over; so attaining what he wants takes on the quality of a life and death issue.

Pluto takes 248 years to travel through the Zodiac. Like Uranus and Neptune, the sign Pluto where it falls in a horoscope represents part of the Zeitgeist of the time. Death and rebirth figure strongly in the sign that Pluto transits. The sign's darker side becomes a cultural problem.

Pluto's transit through Libra from 1972 through 1984 made divorce a common occurrence. The transforming effect was the liberation of women from the traditional structure of marriage. The transit also for all practical purposes brought an end to the diplomatic treaties entered into at the end of World War II when Neptune was in Libra.

Pluto's transit through Scorpio from 1984 through 1995 highlights sex and death. Nuclear accidents, gangs, aids, child abuse, and spouse abuse all fall in its domain. It is hoped that societal attitudes toward sexual preference and the status of women and children as chattel will change by the end of this transit.

With Pluto transiting Sagittarius from 1995 until 2009, religion, philosophy, higher education, and even long-distance travel take their turn being regenerated. Since Pluto brings out the dark side of a sign before regenerating it, scandals involving financial misappropriations and sexual misconduct in religious organizations and colleges will be even more prevalent than they are today. Increased terrorist activity on airlines is another likely manifestation before the world changes its current religious and philosophical tenets. With Neptune in Aquarius at the same time, the birth of a new world religion becomes possible.

Chapter 4

Houses

Each house is ruled by the sign that is associated with it, but signs, houses, and planets are not the same thing. The planets represent the life force. The signs represent how that force manifests, and the houses show the department of life wherein it manifests. The planets, signs, and houses can be compared to a play. The planets are like the actors. The signs are the roles the actors play, and the houses are the stage setting. However, each house carries an overlay of the energy of its ruling sign.

The houses represent the most personal placements in the chart. While everyone born on the same day will have the same planets (with the exception of those that change signs during the day), due to the earth's rotation on its axis, house cusps change degrees every two to four minutes and the house cusps change signs approximately every two hours. The house a planet falls in shows the arena of life it will be concerned with. This is why the priorities of those born on the same day can be so different. While on an inner level these people will be very much alike, their priorities will differ unless they were born at the same time of day and at the same geographical location. Even twins are not born at the same minute.

ASCENDANT AND FIRST HOUSE

The ascendant and any planets falling in the first house represent the face one presents to the outer world. This includes the outer layer of personality, what one is like upon walking into a roomful of strangers rather than friends, and the physical appearance.

It also affects health. Planets found here take on Arian overtones, but these planets function through their Zodiacal sign. A person with a stellium in Pisces in the first house will take charge of his immediate environment, but will do so in a caring, compassionate Piscean way.

SECOND HOUSE

The second house shows a person's earning capacity and how she handles money, despite what the rest of the chart might imply. Personal planets found here receive an overtone of Taurus' concern for money, possessions, and security.

When the Sun falls here, a person's identity is tied to how much money she makes. If Neptune falls here, money will slip through her fingers. She will not know where it goes (without a great deal of learned effort), even if she's a Cancer with the Moon in Taurus and has a tremendous need for financial security.

THIRD HOUSE

The third house, whose ruler is Gemini, rules, along with Mercury, communication including writing, speaking, and what one pays attention to in the day-to-day environment. It also rules early education, neighbors, and short travels. It rules siblings in general, but the next youngest sibling in specific.

Planets found here take on Gemini's restless nature. Those who have a planetary emphasis here have trouble sitting still; they need activity. They are likely to spend a lot of time in their cars driving around town.

An emphasis here also heightens one's intellect. Third house planets enhance left-brained intellect that IQ tests measure.

FOURTH HOUSE

The fourth house rules either the mother or father, the home, family life, and real estate. This house, along with the tenth house, shows how a person was brought up and the effect of early conditioning. It rules both the beginning of life and the end of life, accentuating the tendency for people to end life as they were indoctrinated in the beginning.

A planetary accentuation here heightens the importance of family life along with a Cancerian need for security and a home base from which to operate in the world. The image of a fourth house person hiding at home is overrated. It simply means a person needs to feel secure in her environment before stepping forward.

FIFTH HOUSE

The fifth house rules love affairs, self-expression, creativity, and play as well as gambling and speculation. It rules children in general, but specifically one's first child. It also rules the second youngest sibling.

Since this is Leo's natural house, planets found in this sector take on the Leonine quality of drama and the desire for attention. A planetary emphasis says, "I have to be me." What "me" is depends upon the planets and signs involved. Frequently, people who are self- employed in creative endeavors have an accentuated fifth house.

Love affairs, serious as they might be, as a fifth house expression involve two people who are "playing" together. Compromise and partnership don't come along until the seventh house.

SIXTH HOUSE

The sixth house rules daily work as distinguished from the tenth house of career. It also portrays one's willingness to serve as well as the service received from others.   For instance, a company manager's boss is described by the tenth house, his day-to-day job and the people he manages are shown by the sixth house.

This house also rules health.   Planets found here take on Virgo overtones of fastidiousness and discrimination.   A planetary emphasis here heightens workaholic tendencies and the likelihood that stressful cycles will result in health problems.

SEVENTH HOUSE

The seventh house represents marriage, partnerships, one-to-one relationships in general, and open adversaries. (The implication that open adversaries come from significant relationships deserves thoughtful consideration.)

The seventh house conveys Libra's overtone of cooperation. This distinguishes love affairs of the fifth house--where two people remain individuals-- from marriages in the seventh, where they must compromise if they are to get along. Living together is a seventh house relationship if two people make a commitment to be with one another, a fifth house relationship if they are only concerned with their personal enjoyment.   This house rules the first marriage specifically.

Planets in the seventh house tend to be projected onto the partner rather than seen as part of the self.   When the Sun or Moon or a planetary emphasis is found in this sector, a person tends to lose himself in significant relationships. He becomes "we." While the Moon and Venus for a man, and Mars and the Sun for a woman, describe their ideal mate, the sign on the cusp of the seventh house and planets therein and their rulers describe the actual mate they get or the role they get their mate to play.

The usual definition of this house, limiting it to marriage or business partners, is too narrow. The seventh house describes all one-to-one significant relationships. This includes good friends, co-workers of equal status, and professionals that one hires for advice such as lawyers or astrologers.

EIGHTH HOUSE

The eighth house represents what a person gets from relationships--from sex to joint finances, loans, inheritances, and insurance. This house also rules death, occult interests, and the astral plane.

Scorpio's overtone falling on planets found here gives them greater depth, intensity, and emotionality. Those with this house emphasized frequently experience a death of someone around them at an early age that profoundly affects them. They develop a life-long interest in reincarnation. Like Scorpio, they also want to understand the underlying meaning of why things are the way they are.

Just as frequently, these people end up in positions of dealing with other people's money.

Planets found here influence attitudes toward sex and as well as sexual desires.

NINTH HOUSE

The ninth house rules higher education, one's philosophical or religious view of the world, and long distance travels. It also rules the second spouse and the third child.

Planets here have Sagittarius overtones which can vary from a wanderlust for foreign places to setting up a philosophical construct for how the world should operate. The importance of higher education cannot be overstated when this house is accentuated. These people judge themselves by their degrees.

An emphasis here, like one in the third house, usually indicates a highly developed intellect. When relational planets such as the Moon or Venus fall here, an attraction to people from other cultures exists.

MIDHEAVEN AND TENTH HOUSE

The tenth house, along with the fourth, represents the family axis and may describe either the father or the mother. It also describes one's professional status, career, public standing, and relationship to authority figures, including one's boss.

Planets found here take on the Capricorn overtones of seriousness, hard work, discipline, and responsibility. Those with this house emphasized must be in a position of power and authority in order to be fulfilled. They want to be looked up to and respected.

The seventh and tenth houses are the most visible houses in the chart. Those with a predominance of planets here get attention easily. This makes it easier for them to get ahead if they are doing "what they are supposed to," or to get in trouble if they are not.

ELEVENTH HOUSE

The eleventh house rules goals, friendships, and group activities. Planets here take on Aquarian overtones. In youth those with a planetary emphasis in this sector are strongly influenced by their peers, but as adults they become the ones doing the influencing. Yet, they want to belong to some group, organization, or association of like minded people, working for a cause or ideal that they believe in.

Strong loyalties exist in friendship when this house is accentuated, and a spouse or lover never displaces friends. If the Sun, Moon, or Venus is found here, a lover must be a best friend if the relationship is to survive. Also, friends can become lovers, and old lovers can become friends.

TWELFTH HOUSE

The twelfth house is traditionally called the "house of self-undoing." It rules hospitals, prisons, confinement, and secret enemies.

This house rules the subconscious or unconscious as well as psychic ability and spiritual ideals. Planets found here are hard to identify with because they operate behind the scenes and are not consciously integrated into one's life, although their characteristics may be clearly visible to others.

Twelfth house planets have Pisces overtones of sensitivity, caring, compassion, and naive idealism. Those with a planetary emphasis here frequently do not want to live on earth. They long for a more Heaven-like environment, despairing that the world does not meet their ideals. At their extreme, the people prefer to retreat from the world. Even when well adjusted, they are more comfortable working behind the scenes in any endeavor.

Chapter 5

Aspects

Planets that aspect each other form relationships in which the expression of their energies becomes intermingled. The ease or difficulty of this intermingling depends upon the nature of the planets and the type of aspects. Ease and difficulty should not be confused with good and bad.

Harsh aspects push a person to grow, to change. They stimulate activity. Favorable aspects connote ease. The planetary energies combine naturally. Harsh aspects push a person to do something. When the aspects are favorable one may do the same thing, but he does it willingly, without feeling pressured. At the extreme, a chart with all easy aspects can give a person license to do what he wants, regardless of the morality, because he does not expect any negative consequences.

Most charts have a combination of favorable and unfavorable aspects. While it is impossible to turn difficult configurations into harmonious ones, successful living comes from balancing contradictory needs as defined by the planets involved rather than trying to choose one need over another. This entails a strong degree of personal awareness. Many people don't recognize that this internal conflict can be reconciled. They are more likely to believe that that's just the way it is, or they see the problems as manifestations of the world around them rather how that world reflects their own psyche.

CONJUNCTION ☌

The conjunction takes place when two or more planets fall within an eight-degree orb of each other. Since the aspect starts at 0 degrees, it has an Aries connotation of beginning that represents a dynamic, intense union of planetary energies. When the planetary energies combine harmoniously, this union gives greater strength to each one. An inharmonious combination puts the planets into conflict for supremacy. The individual must then learn to unite their energies giving them equal weight.

DIFFICULT ASPECTS

Harsh or difficult aspects come in multiples of two.

OPPOSITION ☍

The first division of the circle is the opposition, which has 180 degrees and divides the horoscope in half. It connotes confrontation, conflict, polarity, pulling apart, or separating. Frequently, the opposition is experienced in an I - Thou way, symbolizing the Aries - Libra polarity. The conflict it brings seems to come from the outer world or another person rather than from oneself.

This aspect requires awareness to balance the opposing forces as expressed by the planets and ways of being as expressed by the signs (usually opposite) they fall in.

SQUARE □

The square has 90 degrees and divides the circle in four. It also connotes stress and conflict between planetary energies. The difference between the square and the opposition is that the square takes place internally. It's as if the planets involved are fighting with each other on an internal level and pulling in cross directions, creating a sense of being boxed in. Squares are dynamic because they force a person to take action to resolve internal conflict. They usually occur between signs in the same quadruplicity.

SEMI-SQUARE, SESQUIDRATE

The semi-square, which has 45 degrees and the sesquiquadrate, which has 135 degrees, considered minor aspects, both represent a division of the circle by multiples of eight. They share the tension of the square and opposition but in ways that are harder to define. Simply thinking about them as conflict or internal tension is the easiest way to work with them.

FAVORABLE ASPECTS

The easy or favorable aspects divide the circle by three. They represent a harmonious blending of planetary energies.

TRINE △

The trine is 120 degrees. It represents a division of the circle by three. It's the most favorable aspect. Trines depict natural talents one does not have to work for as they bring forth an easy energy flow between planets. Trines represent things that tend to fall in one's lap. They are lucky.

SEXTILE ✶

The sextile is 60 degrees and represents a division of the circle by six. Since six is a product of three and two, it combines the trine with the opposition. It's still favorable but it requires more effort than the trine to combine the planetary energies.

EXCEPTIONS

The quincunx and the semi-sextile are exceptions to the harmonious energy of the three-fold division.

QUINCUNX ⚻

The quincunx or inconjunct is 150 degrees. While it is a multiple of three, it is not a favorable aspect. The quincunx represents the combination of two signs that have no basis for a relationship with each other. Exactly how it works is hard to define. While it's usually given a sixth-or-eighth-house connotation, simply defining it as tension that requires adjustment rather than limiting it to work or health or death seems to produce more accurate results.

SEMI-SEXTILE ⚺

The semi-sextile also represents the division of the circle in multiples of three. It is 30 degrees. The semi-sextile is often considered mildly favorable, but that does not turn out to be the case in practice. Since it, like the quincunx, unites two signs that do not relate to each other, their energies do not mesh well.

ORBS

For all major aspects, an eight degree orb is used. For all minor aspects except the quincunx, a two degree orb is used; three for the quincunx. Translation of Light is taken into consideration. This means that if the Sun is at one degree of Aries, the Moon at five degree of Libra, and Jupiter at ten degrees of Capricorn, the Sun will be square Jupiter because the Moon translates light between them.

Chapter 6

Elements.

Starting the chart by considering the elements first gives the client information he can readily identify with and allows him to become comfortable before hitting more difficult points in the horoscope.

Fire, air, earth, and water represent four distinct ways of perceiving the world. No chart contains only one element, so this world view becomes a mixture of those represented. Each element has its inherent strengths and weaknesses.

The elemental balance in a chart is determined by counting the number of planets, along with the ascendant, in each element and then weighing whether the planets are personal or outer. Personal planets convey a stronger emphasis since they are tied to an individual's identity. The outer planets describe the Zeitgeist when one is born. While two planets in two elements and three planets in the others represents a numerical balance, this does not necessarily constitute an elemental balance. Two outer planets and no personal planets in an element constitutes a lack if the ascendant does not fall in it.

FIRE

The fire signs, Aries, Leo, and Sagittarius, represent the spark of life. Fire is the most positive of all the elements. With spontaneity and enthusiasm, fire signs directly pursue whatever inspires them. These signs are internally, not externally, motivated. They have their own sense of truth. Even when their desires coincide with what society tells them they are supposed to want, those desires stem from within.

Fire signs want life to be an exciting adventure. They want to conquer the world. Their dreams focus on the possibilities of what can be. Fire signs like to think they are logical, but they function more on instincts than they care to admit. They intuitively look into situations and decide, "yes, this is for me," or "no, it's not." Likewise, fire signs are also more emotional than they'd like to believe, although they feel more comfortable expressing positive or outgoing emotions like enthusiasm or anger than negative ones like sadness.

A person with a fire sign emphasis has zest, enthusiasm, spontaneity for life. He can jump up and down from excitement upon hearing good news when he's by himself--he doesn't need an audience. However, in all likelihood, he needs to learn patience, that he can't always have or accomplish what he wants at a given moment, and that the world does not function on his sense of timing.

On the other hand, people who lack fire tend to be lethargic. Not only do they not jump up and down, it's hard for them to get going at all. They do not express enthusiasm easily.

EARTH

The earth signs, Taurus, Virgo, and Capricorn, possess a practical, material approach to life, accompanied by a strong need for financial security. They are externally motivated and relate to the world through their senses, wanting to see, feel, taste, and touch, before they believe something exists. Give them tangible evidence and common sense reasoning. Earth is not interested in theory, abstractions, or what sounds like a good idea. They want to know if an idea can be put to work. Otherwise, it's of no use.

Earth is a stable element. Disliking change, earth signs approach life conservatively. They excel at handling day-to-day matters such as money, responsibilities, and the demands of the material world. Patience and discipline come naturally. Hard work presents no problems, but they must be wary of the tendency toward narrow-mindedly sticking to what they know rather than seeing the larger picture.

Because of the emphasis on earth's conservative side, don't underestimate the earth person's sensual nature--earth is the most physical element. While earth signs (with the exception of Taurus) generally do not like a public display of affection, what goes on in private represents an entirely different matter.

Those who have the element of earth prominent in their charts have no trouble dealing with the realities of everyday life. Motivated by a need for security, their common sense approach to situations makes it easy for them to handle the demands of the material world.

Those whose charts lack earth are not motivated by practical concerns. This does not necessarily mean they are uninterested in money or material possessions, but rather that they are not motivated by a desire to accumulate them. Their capacity for practicality will be determined by the strength or weakness of Saturn's placement.

AIR

The air signs, Gemini, Libra, and Aquarius, face life through their intellect. They want A + B to = C and are not comfortable when it does not. Air signs view situations from a detached perspective. This allows them to be rational in the midst of turmoil. They are objective, logical, and need explanations; but unlike earth, these explanations need not be tangible, just reasonable. Because of this, air signs must be careful of thinking a problem is solved once they come up with the idea for a solution or that something is accomplished because they thought of it.

Air signs are outgoing and positive, but they do not jump into experience as readily as fire. They think before they act. They excel at planning and organizing ideas, original thinking, writing, and speaking--all forms of communication. Intellectually curious, they go on learning forever.

People with a predominance of air signs relate well to other people, mind to mind. They are lively, entertaining conversationalists and enjoy the sharing of ideas. But relating heart to heart is more difficult. Air has a cold side that blocks out emotions. They'd rather think than feel. At their worst they can be insensitive or even cruel. Intellect does not necessarily leave room for empathy or for recognizing the emotional needs of others or oneself.

On the other hand, those who lack air lack the capacity for detachment. They become totally immersed in whatever they are involved in and cannot stand back and objectively observe.

WATER

Water is the most feminine of the elements. To the signs Cancer, Scorpio, and Pisces, feelings are real. They are internally motivated and rely on their instincts to make decisions. They judge people, situations, or ideas by how they feel about them.

Water signs cannot rationally communicate how they know what they do. All they experience is very personal. Situations do not happen around them, but to them. They feel interconnected with their environment and perceive undercurrents in people and situations that the other elements miss.

Empathy, compassion, and emotional depth come easily. Water signs protect and nurture others and want the same in return. They have a strong need for emotional security. They do not jump into action. They want to feel comfortable and familiar first.

People with a water sign emphasis face life through their feelings and emotions. They trust their instincts. They don't need reasons; they just know. Their sensitivity can be a double edged sword. They perceive the undercurrents in their environment, notice things that others would overlook; but at the same time their environment affects them. They pick up the moods and vibrations of those around them and sometimes cannot distinguish between those moods and their own.

Those who lack water do not lack emotions. Every chart has a Moon, which symbolizes feelings, regardless of what sign it is in. But those without water find it difficult to allow themselves to feel and have little understanding of the feelings of others.

Chapter 7

Quadriplicities

The quadriplicities, cardinal, fixed, and mutable, further define a person's approach to life. A balanced approach occurs when the ten celestial bodies fall just about equally among the quadriplicities.

CARDINAL

Cardinal signs, Aries, Cancer, Libra, and Capricorn, like activity. Sitting still is not one of their strong points. These signs are the initiators of the Zodiac, but their initiation takes place in different domains.

Cardinality is frequently thought of as the element of fire or the sign of Aries only. Aries initiates anywhere, but Cancer takes action where she feels secure, whether that's the home or in any other environment in which she feels comfortable. Libra displays initiative in relationships and in dealing with people. Capricorn takes precedence in business and practical matters.

Cancer and Capricorn are receptive signs even though they are cardinal. What these signs have in common is that they excel at starting things, they need activity, and have a low tolerance for boredom. Whether or not they finish what they start will depend upon the rest of the chart.

Those who have a preponderance of cardinal planets function best in start-up situations. They like to get things going. Ideally they arrange their lives so that they can continually move on to new challenges. Maintaining a routine is not one of their strong points.

For those who have two or fewer planets in cardinal signs, starting something new can seem like speaking a foreign language. They almost don't know how to do it. The first step in any endeavor is the hardest for them; and it's where they need to push themselves the most. If they wait until they're comfortable and want to proceed, they'll be waiting for their next lifetime. For some people this represents the key to their life's biggest problem. Recognizing this allows them to acknowledge their discomfort and move on from there.

FIXED

The word, fixed, conveys a perfect image of the fixed signs, Taurus, Leo, Scorpio, and Aquarius. These strong willed signs are motivated by their own sense of principles. They do not like change. They preserve what they are familiar with.

For Taurus that means everything, particularly money and possessions. For Leo it means whatever his heart is set on, for Scorpio whatever she becomes emotionally involved with, and for Aquarius, his ideas and ideals. These goal-oriented signs finish what they start by persisting and persevering despite the odds. They make good managers.

Those with a preponderance of planets in fixed signs find it difficult to reevaluate once they take a particular course of action. They finish what they start even when they shouldn't. These signs need to learn when to get out of situations, whether a job or a marriage, rather than persevere. Change means crisis to them, even when the change is positive.

Those who lack fixed planets have trouble completing projects. They initiate with the best of intentions but quickly lose interest.

MUTABLE

The mutable signs, Gemini, Virgo, Sagittarius, and Pisces, are flexible. In any environment they adapt and make changes they deem necessary. This makes them appear easy to get along with. Mutable signs are concerned with ideas.

Gemini is concerned with rational thinking. Virgo uses information to put the material world in order. Sagittarius tends toward the philosophical plane, while Pisces focuses on a spiritual ideal.

People with a preponderance of mutable signs may find their lives adrift since its easier to switch or move on than fight for what they want. Those who lack mutable planets find it difficult to change--even when change will benefit them. They also find compromise difficult, regardless of the necessity.

QUADRUPLICITY BALANCE

In a chart where the quadriplicities are balanced, a person comes up with ideas which are mutable, puts them into action which is cardinal, and completes and maintains what he begins, which is fixed. When one or more of the quadriplicities is under emphasized, a person has problems in those that are under and over emphasized.

Those with a cardinal emphasis who lack fixity are great initiators, but have trouble finishing what they start. Even when they succeed in finishing, they tend to keep initiating change, despite what is needed. The entrepreneur who starts the business but cannot meet the stockholders' expectations typifies the cardinal personality--because the skills it takes to originate radically differ from those it takes to maintain. Cardinal people need to learn not to fix what is not broken or to move on to the next project making sure they've placed a good manager in charge of the last one.

Those with a fixed emphasis finish what they start. While they are good at preserving and maintaining, if they lack cardinal planets, they have problems getting started. The first step is always the hardest for them. While these people seem to have trouble completing projects, in reality, they have trouble starting, so there can be no completion.

People with a preponderance of planets in fixed and mutable signs adjust to what they become familiar with. They have difficulty making changes since change requires initiation. They tend to stay in bad situations too long and need to learn when to get out.

People who have a cardinal and fixed emphasis not only initiate, but finish what they start. If they lack mutability, they find adapting difficult. They want to get situations going and keep them going their way. They need to be wary of refusing to make changes that would be beneficial because the ideas were not theirs or they are unfamiliar with the process.

Those with a preponderance of planets in mutable signs are good at coming up with ideas. With the exception of earth sign, Virgo, they work best in the theoretical realm and are happiest when they do not have to deal with putting their ideas into action. If mutability is balanced with cardinality, they can take action. If they lack fixity, they must push themselves to complete what they start or learn to give it away to someone who will.

While all this may sound self-evident to astrologers, for many clients a light bulb goes off when they hear it. Those who lack cardinality recognize that they may never feel comfortable in starting--so they can stop waiting for that day. Their choice is to give up at the beginning without trying or to push through their resistance to initiation. Those who lack fixity realize they never feel like finishing anything. They're easily bored. If succeeding is important enough to them, they'll have to learn to tolerate this boredom, or find someone else who can complete what they start. Those who lack mutability must learn that change is inevitable and that everyone must adjust some time, whether they like it or not.

Chapter 8

Ascendant

Since the ascendant represents the exact moment of one's birth--the most personal point of the horoscope--it's a fitting place to begin delineation of the personal placements. The ascendant's characteristics are most visible during youth, although, like the rest of the chart, it stays with one for a lifetime. The Sun, on the other hand, represents one's basic identity, and its sign displays the qualities that a person grows into over a lifetime.

The ascending sign portrays the face one presents to the outer world. It is the mask or persona that one is born with rather than a mask one consciously chooses to put on. This outer layer of personality shines through most visibly in new situations, such as the way a person acts upon entering a roomful of strangers rather than how he appears in a roomful of friends.

Along with any planets occupying the first house or the twelfth house conjunct the ascendant, its sign projects the image that others first see. This includes one's physical appearance. When the ascendant radically differs from the rest of the chart, what others see initially is not what they later get.

People with fire or air signs rising move positively into new experiences. They join in what's going on around them and generally appear self-confident regardless of the rest of the chart. A person with Aries rising jumps into the unknown even if he happens to be a Cancer with a fourth house Sun.

Conversely, people with earth or water signs rising tend to take a back seat in new situations. They wait to feel comfortable or to see what will happen before they join in. They act this way regardless of how assertive the rest of the chart may be. While an Aries with a tenth house Sun and Cancer rising is likely to rise to a leadership position, at an early age she will hide behind her mother, and as an adult she will still hesitate before jumping into unfamiliar territory--waiting to feel comfortable.

The way in which each rising sign faces new experiences, irrespective of the rest of the chart, is as follows:

Aries Rising courageously jumps into new experiences with spontaneity, enthusiasm, and frequently little forethought. He represents the true individual, the pioneer riding off into the sunset. He desires to be in a position of leadership because the leader gets what he wants, and Aries Rising never wants to be told what to do or how to do it. Others see him as fearless, direct, and assertive or pushy and abrasive.

Because **Taurus Rising** loves her comforts and pleasures and places a strong emphasis on security, she hesitates before taking action in unfamiliar situations. Others initially see her grace and charm or her potential for inertia. Recognizing her stubbornness comes later. (Taurus' motto is "Let's not fight about it, let's do it my way.")

Gemini Rising presents a friendly, outgoing exterior. Being able to converse with almost anyone on almost any subject, he meets people easily and fits into any social setting. Others see Gemini Rising as fun, intelligent, and easy to get along with, or as a flighty "air head."

Cancer Rising mothers those around her. She's sensitive to the emotional needs of others and expects them to be sensitive to hers in return. In unfamiliar territory, she hesitates, wanting to feel secure and to know how situations will turn out before entering into them. Others see Cancer Rising as timid or insecure, or mistakenly view her shyness as aloofness.

Leo Rising walks into a roomful of strangers and takes over. He always looks impeccable--or vain--whether he's seen at a formal party or the corner grocery store. His fun-loving spontaneity charms those around him, but his constant need for attention can put people off. Others see Leo Rising as self-assured and confident no matter what the situation.

Virgo Rising analyzes what's going on in her immediate environment with a sharp eye for detail. Before moving forward she wants to find the perfect solution to any problem and doesn't hesitate to let others know what that solution is. Some admire

Virgo Rising's precision and discriminating taste while others criticize her fuss-budget attitudes.

Libra Rising is always socially appropriate. Concerned with relationships and what others think--especially of him--Libra goes out of his way to get along, using diplomacy as his guide. Others become enamored with the Libran charm. Later they may recognize Libra's diplomatic way of getting others to do what he wants while they believe they came up with the idea.

Scorpio Rising prefers to stand back in new situations and survey what's going on. She notices everything around her, whether it's overt or covert. Before joining in, she quietly psychoanalyzes everyone in the room. Scorpio Rising does not know the meaning of the word moderation, and others frequently do not feel moderate about her. Those who perceive her personal power feel strongly attracted or repelled by it.

Sagittarius Rising jumps into new situations with a sense of adventure. He wants life to be fun, interesting, and forever challenging. The challenges may be physical, such as riding horseback through unfamiliar terrain; intellectual, such as finding meaning in a philosophical construct; or adventurous, such as hitchhiking through Europe or Asia. Others can be charmed by Sagittarius Rising's warmth and outgoing nature, or they may see this quest for adventure as irresponsible and childish.

Capricorn Rising is born old and mature. She takes life seriously and assumes responsibility easily. In unfamiliar situations her reserve can border on coldness, but this emanates from her shyness. Capricorn rising has no trouble taking over at a business meeting or once her authority has been recognized. Others perceive her as hard working and dependable on the positive side and cold and rigid on the negative.

Aquarius Rising conveys a friendly, sociable yet independent and individualistic demeanor. His interest in what's new, unusual, and out of the ordinary sets him apart. He joins in groups and social settings easily, but his ideals mean more to him than people. Others initially perceive Aquarius Rising as friendly, outgoing, and easy to be around. Recognition of his stubbornness and dislike of those who disagree with his ideals--particularly the conservatives--come later.

Pisces Rising is more sensitive to her immediate environment than any other sign. She feels the vibrations going on around her whether she wants to or not, and she can have trouble distinguishing those vibrations from her own feelings. This makes being in large groups of people difficult to handle. Others see Pisces Rising as caring and considerate once they get to know her, but her initial timidness makes that hard to do.

Chapter 9

Hereditary Factors (A)
Fourth-Tenth House Axis

While the chart as a whole defines a person's character and potential life experiences, the signs on the cusps of the fourth and tenth houses, their rulers, and any planets found there and their rulers, describe one's upbringing. These placements form the basis of life expectancies.

The myth of a happy childhood is pretty much just that. In seeing hundreds of clients a year, the author rarely finds a chart that indicates a free, frolicking childhood. Perfect parents, like perfect human beings, just do not exist. Parental flaws, as well as their strengths, like family genetics, get passed from one generation to the next. Astrologically, these traits take the form of signs, degree placements, and planetary configurations prominent within a family.

The fourth-tenth house axis itself indicates how the child experiences family life and how that imprint takes form in adulthood. Obviously, this does not portray an objective view of family interactions. Each child's view differs depending upon her own chart. The chart reflects the parents' cycles at her birth. Since these cycles are constantly changing, it's no wonder that each child is born into a somewhat different environment.

A long-standing dispute exists in astrological circles over which house, the fourth or tenth house, represents the mother and which represents the father. In actuality these houses form the parental axis. Sometimes the fourth house describes the mother. At other times it describes the father. Sometimes each parent plays both roles. Sometimes the child is raised by an aunt or grandmother or foster mother, and these houses describe that person. The astrologer can easily ask the client which parent represents the characteristics associated with each house.

The signs on the cusps and planets found in these houses provide a picture of the parents and describe the family's influence. Because the houses are opposite, the signs are opposite, so these houses always provide a polarity. For instance, if Aries is on the fourth house cusp, Libra is on the tenth. This means one parent (Aries) played the aggressive role, perhaps physically, perhaps verbally. In either case the message conveyed was "Go after what you want. Be an individual." The other parent is described by Libra. He represents the conciliatory one whose message says, "Be liked, get along, live harmoniously." These signs convey the polarity in the parents' relationships from the child's point of view, and with opposite signs on each cusp, it's no wonder most children grow up with conflicting messages--and this is only one piece of this puzzle.

Planets found in the fourth and tenth houses, the planets ruling the signs on the cusps and their aspects further complicate the message. Planets found in the fourth or tenth houses show what the family considered important. The parents act out these planets during childhood. The signs show the manner in which these planets are acted out. Planets placed in the fourth house have Cancer overtones regardless of the signs they fall in, while those placed in the tenth house have Capricorn overtones. The fourth and tenth houses set up opposing forces between the home and family and the career orientation. That struggle initially existed in one's family.

The **Sun** in either of these houses shows a strong identification with the family as well as a strong likeness to one parent. The **Moon** in these houses displays an emotional identification with the family. With either the Sun or Moon here, strong family loyalties exist. The ease or difficulty of the relationships depend upon how the Sun and Moon are aspected.

With **Mercury** found here, ideas learned in the family form the basis of one's intellectual framework, as well as showing that ideas were valued within the family structure.

Venus in these houses, if well aspected, portrays a loving family that taught one self-acceptance. If Venus is afflicted, relational problems throughout life will reflect family patterns. (Other patterns in the chart also indicate relational problems--which just about everyone has in one form or another.)

With **Mars** here, assertiveness was taught in the home. Whether that assertiveness was displayed by courage and fortitude such as in overcoming great odds or by aggressiveness, conflict, beatings, or verbal tirades is shown by aspects to Mars. Either way, the family environment was harsh.

Jupiter in either the fourth or tenth houses shows a supportive family environment, where one got whatever he wanted regardless of the family's means. Unafflicted Jupiter here conveys a happy childhood with few demands. If the chart lacks a strong Saturn, the early message that life is supposed to be easy can prove damaging when later life does not turn out as easy as anticipated.

Saturn in these houses, even when well aspected, represents a difficult childhood where the child had a great deal of responsibility and was forced by family demands to act like an adult at an early age. If Saturn is difficultly aspected, love felt like a commodity given in return for living up to expectations--at least from the child's perception. The person must later overcome defining his worth in terms of what he does rather than who he is.

Uranus in the fourth or tenth houses teaches freedom of expression and individuality, many times at the expense of security, especially if Uranus is difficultly aspected. This placement conveys an inconsistent home life, where the child never knows what to expect. He could be rewarded for behavior one day that he is punished for the next. Feeling secure in one's home is difficult with this placement.

Neptune in either the fourth or tenth houses conveys an idealization of family life that one's real family rarely lives up to. These positions coincide with a skeleton in the family closet, whether that be a parent with a drinking or drug problem or prone to mental illness, or one with an inclination to escape from day-to-day difficulties. The message conveyed is, "If you don't look at unpleasant situations, maybe they'll go away." In whatever house Neptune is found, one lacks objectivity.

Pluto in these houses, particularly if harshly aspected, shows dominance and control issues within the family structure. Usually one parent plays the domineering role, and others go along with him out of fear for their survival, irrespective of whether this role is acted out or merely implied.

Difficult aspects to planets found in the fourth and tenth houses show deeply rooted psychological problems that people act out over and over in later life. Easy aspects show how one was encouraged as a child.   Since most charts contain both difficult aspects and easy ones and all have more than one sign or planet ruling these houses, the learned messages are complicated and often conflicting.
The fourth-tenth house axis shows the inconsistent messages learned in childhood. Since

the chart represents one's own nature, the inconsistencies represent what the individual brings forth from his environment, which then reflects what is taught to him within it. This mirror image is very important.

Since the chart defines the child's upbringing, she had to be born into a family that reflects the chart. For whatever reason--fate, karma--the individual chose this type of family life by the moment of birth. This places the ultimate responsibility for working out these issues on the person himself. Blaming the parents provides an easy outlet for an individual's problem. This does not excuse parental flaws that hurt children but it puts them in a more far-reaching context.

Chapter 10

Hereditary Factors (B)
The Moon

The sign the Moon falls in shows how a person expresses her feeling nature, how she mothers or nurtures herself and others, and how she emotionally responds to all situations, not just those considered emotional.

Contrary to most astrological opinion, the author's experience with clients does not indicate that the Moon directly depicts the mother as an individual unless it is tied into the fourth-tenth house axis. Instead, the Moon represents what one learns within the family environment. This learning does not take place consciously. Rather, it represents automatic responses learned unconsciously which do not necessarily coincide with what the family meant to teach. A person with an Aries Moon may learn independence by example from a liberated mother or assertive father, but could just as easily learn to value autonomy by watching a dependent mother or father and unconsciously vowing never to be that way.

WATER SIGN MOONS

The Moon is most comfortable in water signs where it can just "feel." Water signs perceive undercurrents in situations by the vibes. They face life through their instinctive feelings and find truth in these feelings. They possess no need to rationally define where their insights or hunches come from. They just know. For this reason, water sign Moons find it difficult to communicate--particularly about how they feel.

Because feelings, their own as well as others, are obvious to them, they find it hard to believe that others cannot perceive the same way. This is why water sign Moons are often hurt when those they love are not mind readers. They frequently lament, "If you loved me, you'd know how I feel." (This will be less true if the rest of the chart has more rational placements.)

Water sign Moons learned to be feeling in their families. If the Moon receives favorable aspects from other planets, the families understood and rewarded the expression of feelings. If badly aspected, these feelings were stomped upon during childhood leaving deep emotional scars.

Water sign Moons have long memories and can frequently remember in detail anything said and done that hurt them before they reached the age of three.

AIR SIGN MOONS

Air sign Moons want to think about their emotions, not feel them. They want their feelings to be logical. When a conflict arises between thinking and feeling, thinking wins. The problem is that rational judgments do not necessarily alter how a person really feels. This is why air sign Moons send out conflicting messages and can seem so dishonest.

They tell you what they think--because this is what they believe they should feel. They're trying to reform themselves by overcoming their feelings. It's not so much that they lie to other people, but they do not want to admit how they feel to themselves--so how can they admit their feelings to anyone else.

Air sign Moons learned that thinking was more important than feeling as children and that they should be rational above all else. They may have learned this by example from rational parents or as an adverse response to overly emotional parents.

EARTH SIGN MOONS

Earth sign Moons want their feelings to be practical. They are conservative. Emotional expression does not come easily, but they possess a strong nurturing and caring side. They manifest this caring by doing something tangible to express affection rather than whispering romantic nothings in the ears of Significant Others.

Their families taught them to take care of life's practical considerations. But do not underestimate their sensual side. They perceive life through their senses. Not just Taurus, but also Virgo and Capricorn desire physical stimulation.

Earth sign Moons may have grown up in practical families that conveyed a sense of responsibility to them or they may have grown up with totally irresponsible parents from whom they learned the importance of responsibility by negative example. The importance they place on money and material possessions may come from getting everything they ever wanted materially as a child, or it may come from being deprived.

FIRE SIGN MOONS

Fire sign moons, like water signs, just feel. While fire signs don't care why they feel what they do, they're more comfortable with extroverted feelings like joy or excitement than introverted feelings like sadness or even contentment. They can fall in love at first sight and spontaneously express love and affection. They give generously to those they love and expect the same in return. Yet, they still want to be an authority unto themselves.

The emotional message fire signs learned from their family is to be themselves, to express themselves, irrespective of what anyone else says or does. This message may have been learned from watching their freedom-oriented parents, or it may come from growing up with Casper Milquetoast and deciding never to be that way

Chapter 11

How to Proceed

After examining the fourth-tenth house axis and the Moon, the chart itself shows how to proceed. This reflects where the art of astrology takes precedence over the science. Astrology depicts a symbolic language, so it speaks to every astrologer somewhat differently. Each astrologer must find a way to interpret the chart that speaks to her. Ultimately no one right procedure exists, as long as the clients get accurate information that assists them in better understanding of themselves.

All planets, signs, houses, and aspects must be examined. Key configurations such as stelliums by sign or house, planetary patterns like the X-cross, T-cross, or grand trine, or heavily aspected planets show primary emphasis, whether that emphasis is by choice or necessity.

The author examines horoscopes by the way people live, looking at individual priorities, talents and abilities, work and money making capabilities, all relationships, and problems that arise in each of these areas, and how this all combines with a person's value system. The chart as a whole gets attention first, and then gets broken down into departments of life.

Thinking of the entire chart as a play can make it easier to understand. The planets represent the actors. The signs represent the roles they play, and the houses represent their stage setting. The importance of the houses as stage settings can easily be seen by observing people who were born on the same day. Their planets fall in the same signs, but their priorities differ depending upon which houses these planets fall in. The planets take on an overtone of the sign naturally ruling that house. A Scorpio with a fifth house Sun takes on Leonine qualities while a Scorpio with a third house Sun displays Gemini characteristics.

Although the houses represent differing compartments of life, individuals themselves are not so easily compartmentalized. Astrologers examine planets, houses, signs, and aspects; but within an individual, these factors all mesh together. A person doesn't necessarily make distinctions between his thoughts, feelings, and ideas. He has internal conversations that compile all of them, which very likely pull him in differing directions. No human being has a completely consistent nature. The astrologer's job is to put all this into a holistic perspective, recognizing that all parts, including conflicting ones, function. They do not cancel one another out. Rather, they become the source of one's innermost conflict.

In interpreting the chart, the whole must be considered for each piece. In looking at career perspective, while the second, sixth, and tenth houses represent a person's money-making abilities, work habits, and career potential, the signs and planets occupying these houses do not operate alone. His identity as shown by the Sun, his way of thinking as shown by Mercury, and all other planetary placements affect his career potential, no matter where they fall in the horoscope.

The consultation proceeds by addressing major issues. The makeup of the entire chart points out these issues. The way in which these issues affect, or do not affect, specific areas of life gets considered next. It's important to remember that conflict does not arise only from difficult aspects, but occurs whenever contradictory tendencies pull against each other. Signs that are normally considered compatible are not always, and planetary placements that are not angularly related can cause difficulties.

The best way to examine a chart for contradictory tendencies is to assess how differing factors get along. A man with a Taurus Sun wants stability and security; but if he has Venus in Gemini, he also wants variety, change, and not to be trapped in relationships. These two planets do not have to be semi-square each other to present problems. Their contradictory needs present an inherent conflict. This conflict can be acted out in a variety of ways. He may demand relational loyalty from his spouse while having extra-marital affairs himself, or he may choose a fickle partner who acts out the Gemini role so he doesn't have to, or he may be loyal but blame his wife for inhibiting his freedom. Ideally, he will learn to maintain a secure relationship where both he and his spouse retain individual freedom--if only of thought.

Even signs in the same element that are supposed to get along, don't necessarily. A woman with a Pisces Sun and a Scorpio Moon feels conflicting pulls, even though both are water signs. Pisces is kind, caring, sensitive, and forgiving, even when she shouldn't be. She has a strong sympathy for the underdog. Scorpio is intense, passionate, and strong willed. She loves to see people get what they deserve, one way or the other. So, a woman with a Pisces Sun and Scorpio Moon fluctuates between feeling sorry for others and taking care of them no matter what, and feeling outraged by bad behavior and berating herself for being such a soft touch. No matter how this is acted out externally, the internal conversation of these planetary placements will fluctuate between the need to take care of others despite the personal cost and the recognition that those who don't take care of themselves aren't worth knowing. Ideally, this works out with the Scorpio perceptiveness balancing Pisces compassion; but internally there will still be conflict over the right way to be and which action to take. And no matter what she does, she'll feel as though she's missing something.

The next chapter interprets individual charts. The examples chosen illustrate different types of planetary combinations. Two charts represent those of "ordinary people" whose names been changed to protect their anonymity. The other two charts are of famous people to show how their public lives correlate with their horoscopes. Placidius house cusps are used.

The most important points to keep in mind in interpreting the horoscope is that the whole of the chart is greater than its parts, and that differing planetary energies do not cancel one another out. They create inconsistencies that pull a person in different directions. This is normal and all charts, i.e., all people, have these inconsistencies.

Chapter 12

Amy

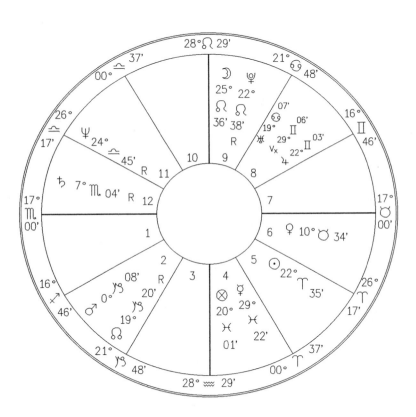

Amy

Amy, was born on April 12, 1954. She is married and owns a business.

Amy has three planets in fire, three planets in water and Scorpio rising, two personal planets in earth, and two outer planets in air. With both her Sun and Moon in fire signs--Aries and Leo--respectively, Amy has great zest and enthusiasm. She doesn't want to miss anything. Her Aries Sun square Uranus reiterates her fire sign desire for life to be an exciting adventure.

Amy has two planets in earth, Venus in Taurus and Mars in Capricorn, so she's not without practicality. These planets represent her pragmatic side, which wants proof before she believes anything, looks for a practical way to get things done, and covets the pleasures of material rewards. They do not do away with the Sun opposing Neptune.

Scorpio Rising and three planets in water portray Amy's emotional side. Her feelings are deep and strong. She perceives subliminally; she reads the vibrations of her environment. Neptune opposite the Sun also enhances this tendency.

Since Amy's two planets in air are outer ones, they do not give the ability to detach and stand back and look at situations objectively. Her earth helps her to be pragmatic, but her strong fire-water emphasizes her instinctive, emotional responses. She's inner-directed and for the most part wants what she wants. She's not motivated by the values of society or by its constraints. Although Aries, Leo, and Scorpio are all very different, they are similar in that they are all strong minded and self-willed.

Amy has four planets in cardinal signs, four in fixed and fixed angles, and two in mutable. Four planets in cardinal signs, particularly those in Amy's chart (a T square with the Sun in Aries opposite Neptune in Libra, square Uranus in Cancer and Mars in Capricorn), denote a strong need for activity. Sitting still is not one of her strong points. She must be on the go. This reinforces her fire signs. She's also good at initiating situations.

With four planets in fixed signs and with fixed angles, Amy not only initiates but, unlike many Aries, she completes what she begins. Her fixed planets give her stamina and perseverance. Moon and Venus both in fixed signs convey strong emotional and relational loyalties. She sticks by people, as well as perseveres in situations.

Two planets in mutable signs do not give her much flexibility. It is natural for Amy to initiate what she wants and keep it going. Change is much more difficult. Learning that she can't always be in control and that life without change is impossible represents one of her strongest lessons. Scorpio Rising and a Moon - Pluto conjunction in Leo reinforce the importance of this lesson.

Amy's Scorpio Rising conveys strong intensity. An "I want what I want and nothing else will do," attitude toward life prevails, which her Moon - Pluto conjunction in Leo and her Aries Sun reinforce. Scorpio Rising lives by passion. Amy's either involved or not interested, whether it's with a person, place, or idea. In new situations, Amy is quiet and somewhat reserved. She stays in the background and views what's going on before joining in. Upon meeting others, she either likes them or doesn't. She lets her instincts makes the choice. As long as she's not emotionally involved or listening to her overly sympathetic side, she's a good judge of character. Her instincts tell her whom to trust and whom not to.

Her fourth-tenth house family axis has Aquarius and Leo on the cusps with Pisces and Virgo intercepted. Mercury in Pisces falls in the fourth house. Three of the four rulers of her parents--Uranus, Neptune, and the Sun--fall in a T-square with each other. Amy was born at a time when her parents were going through marital difficulties, which is shown by these aspects and reinforced by Mercury's out-of-sign square to Mars in Capricorn. Arguments, disruption, unpredictability were all part of the family environment.

These aspects also show that Amy never knew what to expect or how to get approval, which her Leo Moon needs. One day she could be rewarded for behavior that she would be punished for the next. Her Moon in Leo conjunct Pluto conjuncts the tenth house cusp from the ninth house. The emotional message she got from her family was to be noticed, recognized, and important, and to have power and control. She got this message because her family life was so out of control.

Which brings up the T-square. Although Amy has a complicated aspect pattern, there are two main configurations that stand out. The first is the T-square from the Sun in Aries opposite Neptune in Libra, with both square Uranus in Cancer. The second is the trine of the Moon - Pluto conjunction in Leo to the Sun in Aries and their sextiles to Neptune in Libra and Jupiter in Sagittarius, which also sextiles the Sun.

Her T-square falls in cardinal signs. The Sun represents her sense of identity. An Aries Sun is enterprising, independent, and self-motivated. These characteristics helped her to get through her early life. The square to Uranus in Cancer from the Sun heightens her independence and freedom needs: the "I have to be me" way of living. Because the aspect is a square, independence is flaunted rather than just naturally acted out. It's as if Amy has to prove that she's free, presenting problems with authority figures. The opposition of the Sun to Neptune in Libra softens the Aries temperament, just as the square to Uranus heightens it.

The generation of Aries who have Neptune opposing their Sun take on Piscean qualities of softness, gentleness, compassion, and caring, even though these qualities function through an Aries temperament.

The generation of people born with Uranus in Cancer squaring Neptune in Libra have to discover how to meet their freedom needs and their ideals at the same time.

Uranus, at its highest level, frees an individual from constraints so that he can be his higher Self. Neptune, at its highest level, represents the ideals of a heavenly life, including truth, beauty, and the way life is supposed to be, but rarely is, on earth.

Uranus, at its lowest level, becomes rebellion for the sake of rebellion and freedom as license. Neptune, at its lowest level, becomes fog, illusion, deception, and escapist behavior such as drugs and alcohol.

The generation of people born with Uranus in Cancer squaring Neptune in Libras was the one most strongly affected by the break-up of the family as Pluto transited through Libra. Uranus in Cancer functions through the family; Neptune in Libra through one-to-one relationships.

In Amy's case, since her Sun opposes Neptune and squares Uranus, these generational lessons become her own personal ones. She has to find a balance between freedom and independence and her ideals. The way this works for her is that her Aries Sun quickly jumps into the unknown. She is action-oriented and likes adventure and risk-taking. If she's not constantly on the move, she's bored. She's also extremely independent and believes everyone else should be too.

But the Sun opposite Neptune makes her a soft touch. She finds it hard to say no to people who need her, even at the expense of her independence. Her quick actions can lead her to volunteer to take care of others before she's stopped to think about the consequences. This then activates the square between the Neptunian ideals and the Uranian independence. Once she's in the situation, she feels trapped and wants to get out. She's obligated herself; yet she feels as if she had no choice.

All of this is reinforced by her Moon conjunct Pluto in Leo, Scorpio Rising, and her Venus in Taurus opposition Saturn in Scorpio. The Moon receives no difficult aspects except the conjunction to Pluto. It trines her Aries Sun and sextiles Neptune and Jupiter. The Moon in Leo conveys a strong need both to give and to receive love, affection, and attention. Amy needs to be looked up to and appreciated. She's intensely loyal (heightened by the conjunction to Pluto) to those she cares about and will do anything for them provided she feels loved and appreciated.

The Moon's conjunction with Pluto accentuates the need for control and makes her Leo Moon far more introverted and secretive, along the lines of her Scorpio Rising, than it would otherwise be. Her Neptunian need to help others also fits in with her Moon - Pluto power and control needs and the desire to be admired. If she's helping, she's in charge. She has control. Chances are she'll be looked up to and admired. Her Venus - Saturn opposition reinforces taking care of others from another perspective. There's a fear of being abandoned if she does not live up to others' expectations, even though this fear operates on an unconscious level with Saturn in the twelfth house.

In relationships, particularly romantic, the following comes to the forefront. Her Aries Sun square Uranus makes decisions quickly. A fire-water emphasis decides through feelings and instincts.

0104

Romantically, if the chemistry isn't there right away, Amy won't look at anyone twice. And with the Sun opposing Neptune, she's looking for a romantic ideal. Scorpio Rising and the Moon conjunct Pluto in Leo function by passion. She's either in love or not interested, no matter how quickly she decides.

While Amy's cardinal signs cause her to jump in quickly, because of her fixed planets she's in for the long haul. Initially, in a romantic relationship, she puts the her lover on a pedestal. She sees what's wonderful about him. Although it's natural for anyone in love to exaggerate the favorable qualities of her lover or to see him as larger than life, when Neptune is afflicted this exaggeration gets carried to the extreme. Amy has to watch the tendency to ignore anything that even hints of her lover's imperfections.

Afflicted Neptunes operate either by denying the imperfections of a loved one or by not being able to find anyone to love--because no one meets the ideal. Frequently, one person acts out both sides. Conversely, Amy can go from not being able to find anyone she's interested in, to putting someone on a pedestal. Both tendencies ultimately lead to disappointment. Where Neptune is involved, situations look better than they are or worse than they are, but never the way they are.

Amy falls in love quickly and puts her lover on a pedestal. Neptune also creates the desire for romance, which is not the same as love. Leo also wants romance. Venus in Taurus enjoys receiving presents and being taken out to fancy places. In return, Amy takes care of her lover. She goes out of her way to do things he likes--because it makes her happy to see him happy. In the beginning, it looks as though they'll "live happily ever after."

At some point Amy begins to notice her lover's flaws and imperfections and she becomes disappointed. When a person believes another to be the perfect ideal, finding a real human being instead can be difficult to live with. While those who have Neptune afflicted must be wary of getting involved with people who purposely take advantage of them, they also must be wary of setting up the conditions that precipitate being taken advantage of, regardless of whom they're involved with.

A person with a cardinal emphasis without Amy's fixity would jump into relationships, then jump out when her ideals failed to be met. However, her fixity keeps her involved even after she discovers the flaws.

Let's examine her fixed planet needs. Venus in Taurus wants a stable, secure long-lasting relationship. When it comes to love, Amy is not fickle. Because Venus also rules the seventh house of the marriage partner, Amy would choose a spouse with the same relational values. (She did.)

Her Moon - Pluto conjunction and Scorpio Rising add to the intensity of her feelings. When she cares for someone and the relationship is new, she can spend all day thinking about him. Although these placements are intensely emotional, they add an unconscious need for control. The Moon in Leo also needs to feel loved and appreciated. This fits in with the Aries Sun that wants to come first.

The Scorpio Rising and Moon - Pluto combination also gives Amy the belief that she can change or transform anything or anyone. So, when her lover doesn't turn out to be perfect, she'll try to "fix" him up, believing that when she does they will both be happy. These configurations, along with a strong Neptune, make Amy a good judge of people's underlying potential. That's why she's a good judge of character when she's not emotionally involved. However, when she is emotionally involved, she needs to be careful not to confuse a person's potential with what they are actually like. People frequently have great potentials they never live up to. Amy also has to be careful that she does not excuse behavior that she finds unacceptable because she has psychoanalyzed her lover so well that she forgets about his actual behavior and fixates on what she believes to be his underlying motivation. At their worst, strong Scorpio types try to change everyone else so that they can remain the same.

With this combination and the opposition of Venus to Saturn, Amy's feelings are easily hurt. She appears tough and strong, which she can be; but she's also very sensitive. Scorpio always appears as if nothing bothers her, but that's far from true. Leo is the most feeling of the fire signs, and the Moon here needs a great deal of attention and approval.

None of these planetary placements are particularly communicative. Amy has only outer planets in air and practically no planets in houses corresponding to air signs. This makes it highly unlikely that she will talk about her feelings when something bothers her. Scorpio needs time to go off on her own and analyze what's going on, but she has to watch the tendency to obsess about it herself while never speaking to her Significant Other about what's bothering her. The Moon - Pluto does the same.

Venus' opposition to Saturn makes this even more difficult. There's an element of "prove to me you love me" in this aspect. What someone else does for Amy is measured, because she's looking for evidence of caring. Difficult aspects between Venus and Saturn make a person believe at a deep level that they are unworthy of love. Saturn in the twelfth house in Amy's chart and Venus ruling the seventh house of marriage heighten this effect. So while the Moon - Pluto in Leo can be domineering and demanding, and her cardinal T-cross wants to be free, Amy fears being abandoned and needs proof of her spouse's love.

Her relational complaint during her last consultation was that her spouse did not "consider her" enough. What that really meant was that he was not doing what she wanted. He's also been out of town on business a great deal, and she has discovered that she likes his being away. The more he's gone, the more she gets to be free while she still holding on to the relationship.

If her marriage is going to last, Amy must come to understand which of her expectations are realistic. Her husband didn't turn out to be Prince Charming; and while she still loves him, she's disappointed. Her Moon - Pluto conjunction in Leo presents a drawback to working-through the issues because she may value her pride more than her marriage. She doesn't want to admit she's hurt or upset. If her husband doesn't care enough about her to read her mind, she believes he couldn't possibly love her anyway. Because Amy is so good at seeing the underlying meaning in situations and what's left unsaid, it's hard for her to believe her spouse cannot do the same.

The favorable side of her Venus - Saturn opposition ruling the first and seventh house is that she doesn't believe in divorce (although that doesn't necessary mean she won't get one), so she'll try to make the marriage work. Learning how to communicate--to actually talk about her feelings rather than just get lost in them--will go a long way toward helping her to resolve problems.

The same configurations that affect Amy's relationships operate in her career. She's self-motivated, independent, and needs to be free. At the same time she's idealistic and somewhat naive. (Sun opposite Neptune square Uranus.) She also wants to be in charge. (Moon conjunct Pluto.)

Upon receiving a family inheritance, Amy went into business for herself. She has a primarily well-aspected Jupiter in the eighth houses. It trines Neptune, ruler of the fourth house; sextiles her Sun, ruler of the tenth house and conjunct the sixth house cusp from the fifth, and her Moon - Pluto conjunction, found in the ninth house but conjunct the Midheaven. It opposes Mars in the second house, and sesquiquadrates Saturn in the twelfth. She opened a jewelry store where she both designs and sells jewelry. This coincides with her fifth house Sun, Leo Moon, and Venus in Taurus. Having her own business takes away problems with authority figures at the work place.

Amy's out-of-sign grand trine comes into play in the work arena. Her Aries Sun trines the Moon and Pluto in Leo and Mars in Capricorn. Mars is in her second house of money and rules her sixth house of work. This allows her to handle money-making activities and daily affairs practically. Mars, well aspected to both the Sun and Moon, enhances this ability. She makes money easily. Financially, there's an element of luck for her with Jupiter in her eighth house and Mars well aspected in the second. Having her own business satisfies her Aries Sun's need to do things her own way and her Leo Moon - Pluto conjunction's need for control. By being the boss, she gets to be looked up to and respected.

Having her own business also helps her to work out her T- square. It satisfies Uranus' need to be free and do things her own way. It stimulates the positive side of Neptune because she's creating and selling beautiful items. Amy loves her work. She can become so absorbed in a project she doesn't know what time it is or what day it is. Neptune causes a person to lose herself in what she does. When Neptune manifests artistically, works of beauty can be almost effortlessly created.

Eventually Amy will need to deal with her T-square. Even though she owns the store, the necessity of being there conflicts with her need to come and go as she pleases. Venus in Taurus in the sixth house opposing Saturn in the twelfth reinforces this. Although she loves the business, Saturn eventually kicks, and Amy feels restricted.

Lastly, with the favorable aspects to both Mars and Jupiter, Amy has no trouble earning money. However, Mars in the second buys on impulse, particularly when it opposes Jupiter. She needs to be careful of any easy-come, easy-go attitude toward money.

Chapter 13

Janet

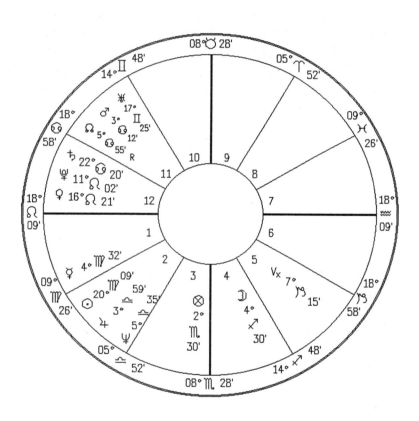

Janet

Janet was born September 13, 1945. She is single.

An examination of the elements shows that Janet has three planets in fire and Leo rising, two planets in earth, two planets in water, and three planets in air. This represents an elemental balance. Her fire planets give her zest and enthusiasm. Her earth planets convey practicality. Her water planets, Mars and Saturn, do not convey the easiest side of emotional expression, but are water nonetheless. Her three planets in air are outer planets so they do not convey as much objectivity as they would if they had been inner planets. However, her Sun and Mercury are in Virgo, and, Virgo, being the most intellectual and air like of the earth signs, reinforces her objectivity.

Janet has four planets in cardinal signs, four planets in mutable signs, and two planets in fixed signs, with fixed angles. Her Sun, Moon, and Mercury fall in mutable signs, so mutable represents her strongest quadruplicity. People with a preponderance of mutable signs are versatile and easily adapt and change. They also tend to go along with the flow of events.

Janet's four planets in cardinal signs convey initiating ability, but less than the number would imply. Her only personal planet in cardinal is Mars in Cancer, which is not the best placement for Mars energy.

Her fixed angles, along with Venus and Pluto in fixed signs conjunct the ascendant, give her the ability to complete things when she becomes obsessive about them. Otherwise, it can be difficult for her to muster up her determination for a long period of time.

Leo Rising gives Janet a strong will and an air of self- confidence. In new situations she has the ability to join in and take over. Her dramatic flair and her sense of humor make her fun to be around. Her Sagittarius Moon heightens this sense of humor. However, Venus and Pluto in the twelfth house conjunct the ascendant add a reserve. She still wants the attention that Leo desires but can withdraw from it at the same time. Pluto conjunct the ascendant adds a Scorpionic overtone. And Scorpio would rather control from the background or behind the scenes (like the twelfth house) than from up front. Venus in Leo but conjunct Pluto also displays this ambivalence. So if Janet gets too much attention, Pluto's energy becomes uncomfortable, and she retreats. When she does not get enough attention, Leo's not happy. With Mars in Cancer and a twelfth house emphasis, Janet retreats rather than fights when she's upset.

Scorpio and Taurus rule the fourth and tenth house respectively, and their rulers, Venus and Pluto, are conjunct the ascendant from the twelfth house. The Moon in Sagittarius falls in the fourth house. The conjunction of the fourth and tenth rulers shows a strong relationship between the parents. The parents function as a unit rather than as separate people in Janet's eyes.

Scorpio on the fourth house cusp with its ruler conjunct the ruler of the tenth and conjunct the ascendant shows one parent to be particularly powerful. This was Janet's mother. She controlled the family, including Janet's easy-going father, with an iron hand. Scorpio at her best is loving and protective; at her worst, she's controlling, despite the circumstances.

Janet's mother fit both descriptions. While this conjunction trines the Moon and receives no unfavorable aspects, its conjunction with the ascendant heightens its power. Janet felt controlled by her mother and while growing up was afraid to confront her. With these planets in the twelfth house, Janet withdrew when there was any sign of conflict. Yet, with the Moon trine these planets, she and her mother still somehow managed to maintain a loving relationship.

The Moon in Sagittarius shows that the emotional message Janet learned from her family was to be free and independent. Interestingly enough she learned this message from her dominant mother. So on one hand her mother controlled and manipulated, and on the other she encouraged freedom and independence. The Moon falling in the fourth house shows strong emotional ties to the family and the unconscious absorption of all that transpired in the home. The Moon's square to Mercury in Virgo shows there were arguments and disagreements within the home that even her powerful mother did not stop. To this day, Janet has strong ties with her siblings. They argue and disagree but also provide much emotional support for each other.

Janet's chart is unusual in that nine out of ten planets fall on the eastern side of the chart. This means she's in charge of her own destiny. Her life becomes what she makes it, for better or worse. People with this strong eastern emphasis tend to be loners. They're quite comfortable doing things by themselves and actually have to stop and think to invite someone else to join them. Venus, ruler of sociability, falling in Janet's twelfth house, heightens that tendency.

The energies of Virgo and Leo do not combine easily. Leo wants to be admired, loved, respected, and to be center stage. Virgo is the worker of the Zodiac, whose main incentive in performing a task is to do it well. Virgo is the perfectionist. Leo would like to believe he's already perfect so there's no need to improve. Virgo analyzes whatever she does with an eye toward improvement. No matter what she does she believes it can be better. At their most positive, the combination of Leo and Virgo can be the star who makes sure she perfects her craft--whether that craft is acting or making pottery.

Virgo's positive traits stem from her analytical ability. Ruled by Mercury, she's the most logical and intellectual of the earth signs, but as an earth sign, she wants to see her ideas put to work. Janet has very good organizational skills. She's good at teaching and training others because of the ability of her Virgo Sun and Mercury to break things down into their component parts. She naturally divides tasks into the steps needed to complete them and can communicate how to do so. Mercury's sextile to Mars heightens this ability.

With Mercury's square to the Moon, Janet needs to be wary of talking too much, so she needs to learn when to stop giving directions to others. This is true when she's not teaching per se. Virgo not only attempts to improve herself, but has the tendency to try to improve those she cares about. Janet has to watch the tendency to offer suggestions to those around her for how they can improve, whether they've asked for her suggestions or not. What Virgo considers helpful others frequently hear as criticism.

This same critical voice tells Janet what she does right and what she does wrong. The most negative manifestation of that voice, when coupled with the pride of her Leo planets, is that she will not try what she does not believe herself to be good enough at. Leo doesn't want to look bad, and Virgo doesn't want to be frustrated if she can't be perfect.

Janet's Virgo Sun squares Uranus in Gemini and sextiles Saturn in Cancer in the twelfth house (its only major aspect). Saturn in the twelfth house creates unconscious fears but its sextile from the Sun allows Janet to act responsibly without necessarily thinking herself to be burdened by those responsibilities. The square to Uranus gives her a strong need for freedom and independence, which she can flaunt. Uranus in the eleventh house gives her friendships with a wide variety of people. This helps her to counter the reclusive nature of Venus and Pluto in the twelfth house.

Mars also falls in the eleventh house. It sextiles Mercury but squares Jupiter and Neptune. The sextile to Mercury helps her communication with her friends. The squares can mean she over idealizes those she cares about, but, being a Virgo, she sees the faults and flaws at the same time.

With all of these placements, Janet has to watch the tendency to look for Prince Charming in relationships. When Mars afflicts Neptune, a woman tends to search for a romantic ideal. Venus conjunct Pluto falling in the twelfth house reinforce this. The fact that these planets conjunct the ascendant make it easier for Janet to consciously acknowledge her romantic fantasies than it would be if they were placed squarely in the twelfth house.

However, another factor becomes a problem in romance. The Venus - Pluto conjunction represents the way in which she loves. She's obsessive, compulsive, and driven when she's in love. There's an "all or nothing" quality. This configuration also reminds Janet of her mother's dominance, a quality she would actually like to assert romantically. At the same time, with her Sun - Uranus square, she wants to be free and independent, not trapped. Her Sagittarius Moon reinforces this need. Yet, the strength of her own feelings can trap her. With no emotional planets in water, she's uncomfortable with her feelings. She'd rather find a pragmatic solution. If she's not careful, this means she'll retreat from romantic relationships--even those she'd like to have--because she's afraid of losing her freedom. She can tell herself that it's not worth wasting the effort since no man ever turns out to be Prince Charming.

Marriage is not essential for everyone, and Janet can be perfectly happy on her own. The issue here becomes: Is she free enough to choose to be with someone when she wants to be? Or does she unconsciously let Uranus prevent her from doing so under the guise of freedom?

Now, let's turn to Janet's job. Her Leo emphasis increases her desire for respect and status. Her Virgo planets make her do whatever she does well, but they create insecurities about being good enough at the same time. The square of Uranus and the Sun shows that Janet doesn't want to be tied to a job. Yet, being a Virgo with the Sun sextile Saturn she works conscientiously at whatever she does. This is particularly true because Saturn rules the sixth house of day-to-day work.

Her Venus - Pluto conjunction affects her relationships with superiors. Venus rules the tenth house. Janet tends to retreat from authority figures, so she's not criticized or overpowered. Ideally, Janet would like not to work at a job at all, but to be free enough to explore her independent interests as shown by Uranus in the eleventh house. If she's ever to do so, she needs to transform the way in which she handles money. Her Virgo orderliness gets lost in financial matters with Mercury, the ruler of the second, afflicted by the Moon, the Sun in the second afflicted to Uranus, and Jupiter and Neptune (which alone would cause financial problems) also afflicted in the second. Janet buys whatever she wants in order to make herself feel better, and she's generous to family and friends whether or not she can afford to be. It makes her happy.

At this point Janet is consciously working on how her Leo - Virgo emphasis and her strong Uranus affect her choices. A person with a strong Pluto--and Pluto conjunct the ascendant is a strong placement even when in the twelfth house--has the ability to transform herself when she has a strong desire to do so. This obviously takes work, but work does not scare a Virgo.

Chapter 14

Jane Fonda

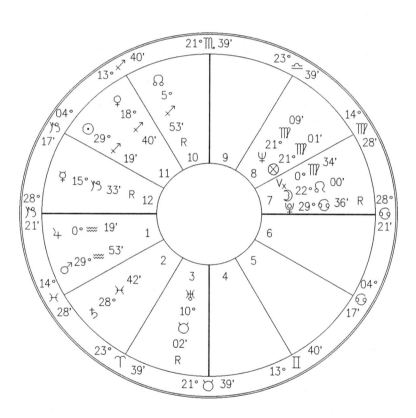

Jane Fonda

Jane Fonda, born December 21, 1937, at 9:14 a.m. E.S.T. in New York City, has been one of the cinema's most controversial actresses. Fonda first achieved fame as a model and an actress, for a time being thought of as a "sex kitten." By the late 1960s she was simultaneously revered and reviled for her protests against the Viet Nam War and on behalf of women's rights, American Indian's rights, and other social concerns. By the 1990s this social protester had turned into a fitness guru and amassed a multi-million dollar empire.

Fonda's chart contains three planets in fire, three in earth, two in air, and two in water. The Sun, Venus, and Moon in fire signs provide her with zest, enthusiasm, and a sense of adventure. With both her Sun and Venus in Sagittarius, she thirsts to know what's around the next corner. A wide grand trine in earth and Capricorn rising add practicality and the ability to make money (despite Neptune's contrary indications). Two planets in air, both in Aquarius, and Aquarius intercepted in the first house, convey logic and the ability for abstract thinking. With only two outer planets in water, emotional expression presents more of a problem.

Her quadruplicities are better balanced. Her four planets in mutable signs help her to formulate ideas. Having a cardinal sign rising and two planets in cardinal signs convey the ability to initiate projects, and her four fixed planets help her to finish what she starts. Thus, she has the ability to come up with ideas, put them into action, and see them to completion.

Fonda has Capricorn rising with Aquarius intercepted in her first house. The rising sign represents the face one presents to the outer world, how one behaves in unfamiliar situations, and the impression one makes on others. This impression gets complicated when an intercepted sign co-rules the ascendant and planets in that sign fall in the first house.

Capricorn Rising forces maturity upon one at an early age. It makes Fonda cautious and conservative in new situations and gives her a pragmatic view of life. Capricorn's ruler, Saturn, square her Sun reinforces this influence. (Neptune opposite Saturn and square the Sun counters this, making her more idealistic--or unrealistic, but Neptune does not do away with Saturn's impact.) The Capricorn influence represents the businesswoman side of Fonda, and very likely severe shyness and self-consciousness were experienced in her youth.

While Capricorn is not a sign usually associated with femininity, some of the world's sexiest women were born under its influence. And since Capricorn excels at learning the rules of whatever game she plays and then playing to win, one way for a woman to win in the 1960s was to become known for her beauty. Being recognized satisfies Fonda's Leo Moon's requirement for attention.

Aquarius co-ruling the ascendant, and Jupiter and Mars in Aquarius in the first house, formulate a completely different picture. Aquarius represents the free-thinking rebel, and a person with Jupiter rising places a high value on her ideals. She must live them, not just pay lip service to them. Mars in Aquarius in the first house endows her with a direct, aggressive nature in going after what she wants, no matter how cautiously she may begin under the Capricorn influence.

The Moon represents the emotional message a person gets from her family. That message may be learned by example, or it may be learned because of what's lacking within the family structure. Fonda's Leo Moon gives her the need to be recognized and to feel important. Fonda's mother was said to be disappointed at her birth; her mother had wanted a son. Fonda's need for attention developed from the lack of it rather than from attention being lavished upon her. The Moon in Leo opposing Mars in Aquarius gives her a volatile temper in response to this treatment and other emotionally upsetting situations.

The fourth-tenth house axis rules one's upbringing. When Taurus and Scorpio fall on these cusps, one's parents can provide stability and security or they can be stubborn and unyielding or both. Since neither Venus nor Pluto have primarily easy aspects, the more difficult side of this combination applies. Pluto, ruler of the tenth, opposes the ascendant almost exactly, and forms a yod with Fonda's Sun and Mars. This portrays one parent as extremely dominating and controlling. Since the seventh house represents the marriage partner, Fonda's first husband will similarly be domineering and controlling.

Venus, the ruler of the fourth house, doesn't fare much better: It forms a trine to the Moon, squares Neptune, and widely conjuncts the Sun and squares Saturn. With regard to the family, Venus square Neptune imagines a fairy-tale family, the way families are supposed to be, but never are. The square to Saturn makes life more difficult. This aspect makes a person feel rejected easily. Love, at an early age, was held as a commodity--"if you live up to our expectations, we'll love you." This sets up a sense of unworthiness--of needing to prove oneself-- that can last a lifetime. So with the Neptune and Saturn influence, Fonda fluctuated between pretending she lived in the ideal family, to being disappointed by cold, distant, and domineering parents. While her Sagittarius Sun helps her to go off independently on her own, her Leo Moon needs significantly more attention.

Fonda's Sagittarius Sun and its ruler, Jupiter, rising give her an optimistic approach toward life, the belief that no matter how bad situations may be today, they'll be better tomorrow. This influence also bestows a craving for adventure and excitement and makes it essential that she stand up for her values. Mars in Aquarius in the first house sextile her Sun reinforces her directness in going after what she wants. With this Mars placement, she won't walk away from conflict; she faces it head on. Her Moon in Leo trine to the Sun provides her with internal harmony--her emotional responses (Moon) reinforce her will (Sun)--despite the circumstances.

Other aspects to her Sun convey problems that she must face. The exact quincunx from Pluto gives Fonda an all-or- nothing approach to whatever she gets involved in. She accomplishes a great deal, whether or not her accomplishments are beneficial to her. Mars in the first house, also quincunx Pluto, reinforces this characteristic, as does Jupiter opposite Pluto.

The Sun square Neptune heightens Fonda's imagination. On the positive side, this aspect increases her creativity. In playing a part, she can lose herself so totally that she becomes the character. On the negative side, this aspect increases her naiveté, making her want to see people or situations as ideal rather than the way they are, which in turn leads to future disappointments. At the same time, the Sun square Saturn implores Fonda to face the reality of the earth plane, to look at the world the way it really is, not the way she wants it to be. On the other hand, this aspect causes her to overdo, based upon the belief that no matter how much she does, she hasn't done enough. This leads her to take on more and more responsibility in order to achieve her ideals without necessarily questioning them.

The generation of people born with Saturn opposition Neptune must grapple to balance their dreams and ideals with their duties and responsibilities. They need to differentiate between the way it's supposed to be and the way it is. Ideally, their choices include both sides of this polarity. When this opposition is prominently configured, these generational lessons become personal ones.

Generally, with this combination, ideals come first. Naiveté leads to disappointment; then reality sets in. Fonda's fierce protestation of the Viet Nam War exemplifies this. Her Sagittarius, Aquarius, and eleventh house emphasis pushed her to stand up for what she believed in. Pluto falling in the seventh house of the public propelled her into the limelight. The idealism engendered by Neptune didn't allow Fonda to see the reality of the War. While her judgments about the U.S. role as an aggressor in what was ostensibly a civil war proved to be far-sighted, her judgments of the North Vietnamese, whom she saw as victims fighting off oppression, proved dreadfully short- sighted. The North Vietnamese savagely butchered the South Vietnamese after the U.S. withdrawal of forces. Many years later, like a true Sagittarius, she acknowledged her mistaken judgment and apologized to Viet Nam veterans, who have yet to forgive her.

Fonda's initial plunge into the fitness industry came from a desire to overcome her own dietary problems. The negative side of Jupiter rising accentuates overindulgence in food and the tendency to gain weight easily, which even the vanity of a Leo Moon cannot completely overcome.

Cancer, which rules the stomach, falls on the cusp of Fonda's sixth house of health. The opposition of Cancer's ruler, the Moon, to Mars explains her turning to bingeing and purging as a teenager to resolve her dilemma with food. When Fonda became pregnant with her first child, she vowed to overcome the bulimia. Her first-house Mars then gave her the incentive to increase her exercise. Her obsessive nature motivated by a strong Pluto increased her will power. This turn of events led to the almost accidental founding of her fitness empire.

Fonda's wide grand trine in earth conveys good business instincts. Mercury in Capricorn provides a practical mind that focuses on getting ahead. Mercury in the twelfth house and trine to Neptune and Uranus makes her thinking intuitive and unconventional and supplies her with an abundance of creative ideas. Fonda's first fitness video became an overnight best seller and pioneered the fitness video market.

Fonda's success can also, in part, be attributed to the many aspects her Midheaven (career direction) receives. Trines to it from Saturn and Pluto hold out the promise of rewards if she puts in effort. A square to it from Mars heightens her aggressiveness in going after what she wants. A square from the Moon accentuates the likelihood of working with women. (Squares don't necessarily signify failure; they show activity.)

At first glance, Fonda's Saturn - Neptune opposition from the second house of income to the eighth house of joint finances does not portend well for money-making pursuits. Saturn in the second can be viewed as restriction in finances. Neptune in the eighth warns of financial gullibility with regard to joint resources or investments. This opposition makes one exacting on one hand and naive on the other. Yet, Saturn in the second does not deny financial reward so long as one is willing to work hard in order to achieve it.

Fonda began the fitness business in order to raise funds for social causes and the political campaign of her then husband, Tom Hayden. She embodied Saturn in the second; she worked hard to make money. Hayden represented the influence of Neptune in the eighth house of joint finances. He spent the money she made to further their shared ideals.

Saturn in her second house trines Pluto, the ruler of her Midheaven, falling in the seventh house of the public. Publicity comes easily to Jane, and publicity sells products. Neptune also sextiles Pluto and Jupiter opposes it. Jupiter - Pluto combinations favor large sums of money. However, it's unlikely that Fonda would have pursued a financial empire without the incentive of funding her social causes. Funding social causes gives her a way of blending the idealism of her fire signs with the pragmatism of her earth signs.

Chapter 15

Senator Edward Kennedy

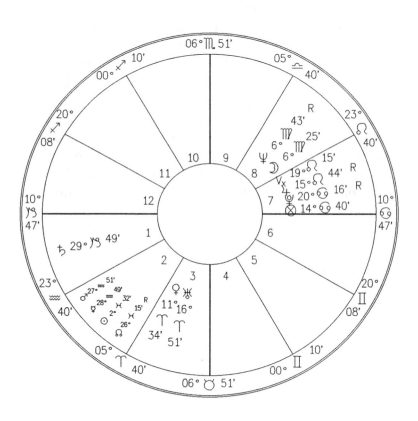

Senator Edward Kennedy

Senator Edward Kennedy was born February 22, 1932 at 3:58 a.m. E.S.T., Boston, Massachusetts. Like Jane Fonda, Senator Kennedy of Massachusetts has been a controversial figure since he first ran for the U. S. Senate in 1962.

In Kennedy's chart, the elements are balanced, three each being in fire and earth, and two each being in air and water. His water planets, including his Sun in Pisces, heighten his sensitivity and feelings. His three planets in fire give him zest, enthusiasm, spontaneity. His Virgo Moon conjuncts Neptune. This conjunction opposes his Mars and Mercury in Aquarius (as well as his Pisces Sun), so his air and earth planets do not give him the detachment and practicality that would normally be expected. Instead, this strongly placed Neptune increases his sensitivity.

Kennedy's quadruplicites are also balanced. Four planets in cardinal signs give him initiating ability; three in fixed, the capability of finishing what he starts; and three in mutable, proficiency at coming up with ideas and adapting to suit the circumstances. This balance can be seen in his know-how in supporting social causes in the Senate. He stands behind his ideals in proposing legislation. Then he works with a wide variety of people with divergent viewpoints in order to pass that legislation.

Capricorn Rising with Saturn in the first house represents the serious, hard-working side of Kennedy. Those with this placement are old and

0131

responsible at an early age. (Much in his chart contradicts this, but doesn't negate it.) Saturn rising usually bestows harsh early conditions. Kennedy, being the youngest of the Kennedy competitive clan, was forced to catch up with the rest of the family.

The Moon represents the emotional message one gets from the family. The message Kennedy received with a Virgo Moon was "be organized, be perfect." A person with the Moon here becomes highly critical of himself. Nothing he does seems good enough in light of the model of perfection. The Moon's conjunction to Neptune simultaneously heightens this tendency and denies it.

The fourth-tenth house axis in the chart describes one's upbringing. Taurus and Scorpio fall on these cusps, and their rulers, Venus and Pluto, form a wide square to each other, with Venus conjunct Uranus. The fourth house ruler, Venus, conjoining Uranus in Aries, conveys instability within the family. This conjunction very well describes both his parents' absence from the home. His mother made frequent trips to Europe. His father was notorious for his love affairs and was often away on business. Pluto, ruling the tenth and falling in the seventh house, also describes a dominant and controlling parent, likely to be the father. The Moon semi-squares Pluto, heightening this dominance emotionally. Jupiter trine Venus and Uranus shows that, although his family life was unpredictable, Kennedy never wanted for anything materially and experienced joy in growing up despite the circumstances. Favorable aspects between Venus and Jupiter represent ease and abundance.

The configuration of Mars in Aquarius conjunct Mercury, also in Aquarius, conjunct the Sun in Pisces in the second house and opposite the Moon - Neptune conjunction in Virgo in the eighth house represents the focal point of this chart.

The Sun personifies one's basic energy. The Sun in Pisces embodies sensitivity, sympathy, compassion, and understanding. Kennedy's stance on social issues typifies Pisces' concern for the underdog. The Mars - Mercury conjunction in Aquarius shows his intelligence, his liberal, intellectual ideals and his willingness to stand up and fight for them. The Mars, Mercury, Sun conjunction as a whole makes Kennedy a much feistier Pisces than would typically be expected, although this feistiness does not do away with his sensitivity. Since this conjunction falls in the second house, Kennedy will spend his own money on his ideals.

The positive side of the Moon in Virgo gives Kennedy practical, analytical, organizing ability, with an orientation toward detail. The conjunction to Neptune heightens Kennedy's already idealistic nature and his sympathy for the underdog. Since this conjunction takes place the eighth house of finances, it reinforces the likelihood that he will invest money he received through inheritance in his ideals.

The signs of Virgo and Pisces are intercepted in this chart. A person has difficulty in youth getting in touch with planets that fall in intercepted signs. Given both the Sun and the Moon falling in these signs, Kennedy had trouble finding himself at an early age. He did not go into politics to fulfill a lifelong ambition, but was compelled to follow in the family footsteps. (Pisces is easily influenced.) After the death of his brothers, politics became the mandatory choice. His Capricorn Rising and first house Saturn propel him into handling responsibilities as well as the idealism engendered by his accentuated Neptune.

Oppositions between Virgo and Pisces represent one of the most difficult opposition axes in the Zodiac. Virgo faces life pragmatically, with both feet firmly implanted on the ground. Pisces sees the ideal, the way things should be. The discrepancy between the way things should be and the way they are can be difficult to live with. In Kennedy's case, this problem is compounded as Pisces' ruler, Neptune, falls in Virgo conjunct the Moon and also opposes Mars and Mercury in the otherwise rational sign of Aquarius. Idealism takes over completely.

Kennedy tries to be the perfect person, perfect in a Virgo sense, but perfect also in an ideal sense. Since no one can achieve perfection, he experiences disappointment with himself as well as with others.

Escapism represents the not-so-favorable side of Neptune. Those with a strong Pisces - Neptune influence find it easier to escape from their pain than to face their problems head-on. Kennedy's escape routes include drinking and womanizing. Neptune rules alcohol. The Moon conjunct Neptune makes one search, and very likely keep searching, for a romantic ideal. This conjunction falling in the eighth house emphasizes the importance of sex. The Venus - Uranus conjunction in Aries further accentuates womanizing.

Kennedy wants excitement and immediate gratification in his love life. Trines of Venus and Uranus to Jupiter in the seventh house expand the number of females readily available for his companionship. The square of this conjunction to Pluto heightens his passion. Since Pluto and Jupiter both fall in the seventh house, these exploits become public knowledge.

With the above aspects of the Moon and Venus, Kennedy finds it difficult to meet one woman who's exciting and romantic enough to satisfy all his fantasies. Yet these same aspects push him to stand up for women's rights. Having a Venus - Uranus conjunction in Aries in the third house of ideas, he believes in the independence and freedom of women. The trines to Jupiter expand this ideal, and the square to Pluto intensifies it.

His Moon - Neptune conjunction opposing the Sun, Mercury, and Mars makes him identify emotionally with all those who suffer and gives him the desire to be of assistance to them. His Capricorn rising, and Saturn in the first house, give him the ability to get his work done despite his personal problems. So, Kennedy works to further liberal social and political concerns. Like a true Pisces with a strong Neptune, he works to better the lot of those who are prejudiced against, such as the poor and minorities. And while he may not have yet saved himself from his personal problems, he works to save others.

BIOGRAPHICAL INFORMATION

Joyce Levine is a professional astrologer with more than twenty years experience. Her training in psychology contributes to her approach to counseling/consulting with clients, who range from individuals, couples, and families to businesses.

She also teaches astrology, meditation, and visualization classes and lectures to astrology associations, professional and business associations, colleges, and cruise ship passengers.

From Joyce's point of view, "Your chart is a picture of your life potential. Recognizing what you do well naturally and recognizing your habitual stumbling blocks puts you on the right track to achieving that potential."

Joyce's clients characterize her as "bringing metaphysical wonders down to earth." And those in the media must agree. She is the only astrologer in the Boston area ever to have her picture on the front page of the Boston Globe as well as the front page of the Living/Arts Section. Joyce has been a guest on radio and television and has been and a radio talk show host.

Joyce is the Past President of the New England Astrological Association, a certified professional since 1979 of the American Federation of Astrologers (AFA), and an Advisory Board Member of the National Council for Geocosmic Research (NCGR) and its Boston Chapter.

Joyce can be contacted directly at 2353 Massachusetts Avenue, #91, Cambridge, MA 02140.

Other Products By
VIZUALIZATIONS
Meditation tapes that can change your life!
Featuring specially designed harp music.
Clear Instructions. Soothing Voice.

<u>Self-Help Series</u>:
Meditation.   Relax. Reduce stress. Become more in tune with yourself. **Side 1** explains meditation. **Side 2** teaches you how to meditate, by taking you through a relaxation exercise and guiding you through the chakras (energy centers of the body), and then letting you drift. It gets you in touch with, and enables you listen to, your inner voice--the voice of your Higher Self.

Creative Visualization. Learn how to consciously use your imagination to create the life you've always wanted. **Side 1** explains what creative visualization is, how it works, and how it can benefit you. **Side 2** guides you through the creative visualization process so that you can begin creating your life the way you would like it to be.

Releasing Anger and Resentment. Release hurtful and upsetting experiences of the past so that you can move on to a positive future of your own choosing. **Side 1** demonstrates the importance of forgiveness and gives you exercises to help you to let go of hurtful past experiences. **Side 2** provides a meditation for letting go. Forgiveness enables you to release the past.

<u>Astrology Series</u>:
Pluto, The Shadow or the Light. Heal yourself, let go of anger and fears, and develop faith in the universe. **Side 1, Integrating Pluto Cycles,** gives you an understanding of what you experience during Pluto's cycle and helps you deal with your unconscious. **Side 2, the Meditation,** takes you through a guided meditation so that you can integrate Pluto's energy into your psyche.

Neptune, Spirituality or Escapism. Unlock your capacity for spirituality, creativity, and love. **Side 1, Integrating Neptune Cycles,** gives you an understanding of what you experience during Neptune's cycles, and helps you unlock its positive side. **Side 2, the Meditation,** takes you through a guided meditation that helps you let go of fog and illusion and create your own images of beauty and spirituality.

Uranus, Erratic Conditions and Upheaval or Freedom to Be Ourselves. Side 1, Integrating Uranus Cycles, helps you discover what true freedom means to you, what to change in your life and how, and where possibilities for breakthroughs exist. **Side 2, the Meditation,** leads you through a visualization leading to a Uraninan type transformation.

Saturn, Handling Responsibilities. Gain wisdom from experience and develop positive karma. **Side 1, Integrating Saturn Cycles,** gives you an understanding of Saturn cycles and what you need to learn from them. **Side 2, the Meditation,** guides you to positive results from Saturn cycles.

The tapes cost $9.95 each. Add $3.00 for shipping up to five products (Mass. residents add 5 per cent sales tax.) Free shipping for more than five products.

ALSO AVAILABLE:
STARSCOPE, THE ASTROLOGICAL NATAL REPORT THAT REVEALS THE REAL YOU
BY JOYCE LEVINE

If you liked this book, you'll love this Report.

Gain a better understanding of why you are the way you are. Your astrological chart as interpreted by Joyce Levine gives you a clear view of what you're like. It reveals your natural talents and abilities, your strengths and weaknesses, how you relate to other people, what motivates you. It helps you determine your inner strengths and recognize the challengers of this lifetime.

Cost $29.95, $3.00 shipping (MA residents add $1.65 sales tax).

To Order send check, money order, or charge account number to
Vizualizations
2353 Massachusetts Avenue #91
Cambridge, MA 02140
617- 354-7075